"Harriette Frances' series of drawings is far and away the most illuminating, as well as exceptionally skillfully rendered, representation of inner states that I know. The progression of images and the accompanying descriptions make it possible to appreciate the depth of her personal experience as well as its universality."

– James Fadiman, Ph.D., Cofounder and Professor, The Institute of Transpersonal Psychology; former Director, Institute of Noetic Sciences. Author, *The Other Side of Haight*

"There is sufficient material here for study by psychoanalysts, psychotherapists, mythographers and art historians as well as all those concerned with the creative process."

– Elinor Gadon, Ph.D., Art Historian. Author, *The Once and Future Goddess.*

"The drawings are complex and masterful renderings of life and death; of personal relationships still in the process of resolving themselves... These drawings demonstrate the very highest quality of line and composition... and form a fascinating record of one woman's journey of search and effort over 20 years."

–Fenton Kastner, Curator Emeritus, The Achenbach Foundation for Graphic Arts, California Palace of the Legion of Honor Museum, San Francisco, California

"These drawings are a form of Classic Surrealism which carries forward traditions borne from the Rennaissance and reiterated in each successive generation from Indo-European artists up to the present time. Owing to this longevity, these works will doubless extend far beyond the present; Ms. Frances' excellent technique renders the work classical by any standard.

As to the message otherwise, Ms. Frances enables us to view renditions of experience in new ways – the result is provocative to mind and heart."

– Michael S. Bell, Art Consultant, formerly with the San Francisco Arts Commission.

"This unique text shows us that the path of self understanding and higher consciousness may not be revealed through words but through images. The author has presented us with the images coming from the depths of the unconscious and has eloquently described their eeventual integration into her conscious life through careful attention to their details.

It is not only an important contribution to the psychology of the unconscious, but a fascinating personal chronicle."

– Elizabeth Osterman, M.D., Ph.D., (now deceased); Emeritus Senior Analyst at C.G. Jung Institute of San Francisco, California

DRAWING IT OUT:
Befriending the Unconscious

(A Contemporary Woman's Psychedelic Journey)

Text and Illustrations by
Sherana Harriette Frances

Introduction by Stanislav Grof, M.D.
Prologue & Afterword by Tanya Wilkinson, Ph.D.

Drawing It Out: Befriending the Unconscious

ISBN 0-9660019-5-8

Copyright © 2001 by Sherana Harriette Frances

Multidisciplinary Association for Psychedelic Studies (MAPS)

2105 Robinson Avenue, Sarasota, Florida 34232

ph. 941-924-6277 ~ www. maps.org

Text set in Adobe Jenson™ with Adobe Galahad™ subheads. Book design: Mark Plummer.

Printed in the United States of America by Data Reproductions Corporation, Auburn Hills, MI

Printed on 60 Lb White Offset Recycled Acid Free paper

"The Mind is its own place, and in itself
Can make a heaven of hell,
a hell of heaven."
–Milton: *Paradise Lost* (1667), Book 1, Line 253

About the Author:

Sherana Harriette Frances is an award-winning painter and printmaker whose work has been exhibited in the three major museums in San Francisco and other national and international museums and galleries. She is represented in the permanent collection of the Achenbach Foundation for Graphic Arts, California Palace of the Legion of Honor, San Francisco, and sits on the Board of Directors of the California Society of Printmakers. Ms. Frances has also studied music therapy at the Transformational Sound School, in San Francisco, with Don Campbell (Founder, Institute of Music, Health and Education, Boulder, Co., and author of *The Mozart Effect*), and has pursued concurrent careers as an art teacher, legal secretary, partner in a bookstore and as the Founder/Director of "Artist's Proof Graphics Workshop" in Marin County, where she continues to print her original lithographs.

Her transformative experience while participating in research with LSD at the International Foundation for Advanced Study in Menlo Park, Ca., in the early sixties, and the life-changing events that it set in motion, was the inspiration for the drawings in this book. Dr. Stanislav Grof has used Frances' dramatic artwork for many years in his training sessions and workshops in Holotropic Breathwork around the world, noting that her expressive drawings are among "the best visionary art I know of anywhere in the world."

Sherana Harriette Frances is the mother of two adult children and grandmother of four. Her hobbies include belly-dancing with the troupe "Dancers of the Desert", exploring books on quantum mechanics, and listening to music. She currently resides in the Bay Area of San Francisco, California.

Dedication:

For Mitchell and Stephanie, Survivors…

With all my love, Mom

Drawings from Series 1 were previously published in the following:

MacLean's, Canada: "The Heaven and Hell Drugs" (June 20, 1964; Vol. 77, 12; pp. 9-13).

Ramparts Magazine, San Francisco, CA: "LSD Journals of an Artist's Trip" (April 1966; Vol. 4, 12; pp. 49-50).

MD Magazine, USA Issue: "LSD-Alarums and Excursions" (September 1966; Vol. 10, 9; p.111).

Print Magazine, New York, N.Y.: "A Graphic Artist Depicts Her LSD Trip" (January/February 1967; Vol. 21, 1; pp. 18-21).

LSD in Psychotherapy & Alcoholism, Edited by Harold A. Abramson, M.D.; Bobbs-Merrill Co., Inc. (1967; pp. 528-529).

Psychedelic Art, Robert Masters and Jean Houston; Grove Press, New York, N.Y. (1968; p. 158).

Beyond Death: The Gates of Consciousness, Stanislav Grof and Christina Grof;
   Thames & Hudson, Inc., New York, N.Y. (1980; pp. 66-67).

LSD Psychotherapy, Stanislav Grof, M.D.; Hunter House Inc., Publ., Pomona, CA (1980; p. 172).

Shaman Woman/Mainline Lady: Women's Writings on the Drug Experience,
   Edited by Cynthia Palmer and Michael Horowitz; Wm. Morrow and Company Publ., New York, N.Y. (1982; p. 177).

Verdensbilleder Magazine (90.1), Johs. Fabricius: Denmark Radio Publishers, Copenhagen, Denmark (1987; pp. 34-35).

The Spirit of Shamanism, Roger Walsh, M.D., Ph.D.; Jeremy P. Tarcher, Inc., Los Angeles, CA (1990; pp. 64-68);
   also *The Spirit of Shamanism*, Japanese Edition, 1996, publ. by arrangement with Jeremy P. Tarcher, Inc.,
   of G.P. Putnam's Sons through Tuttle-Mori Agency, Inc., Tokyo, Japan (pp. 90-94).

Sisters of the Extreme, Edited by Cynthia Palmer and Michael Horowitz; Park Street Press (Inner Traditions),
   Rochester, VT (2000, pp. 173-175).

LSD Psychotherapy, (Revised) Stanislav Grof, M.D.; Multidisciplinary Association for Psychedelic Studies (MAPS)
   Sarasota, FL (2001, pp. 193-194).

ACKNOWLEDGEMENTS

This book originated as a wordless visual dialogue between my conscious and unconscious mind, catalyzed by my experience with LSD, for which my drawings served as a tool for bringing deep underlying issues to my awareness. Without the encouragement and help of many friends and supporters who believed I had an important story to tell, I would not have attempted to put words to the experiences related in this book.

First of all, my thanks to the people at the international Institute for Advanced Study in Menlo Park, California, who insisted on a "report" of my LSD experience there, which in my case turned out to be the first series of drawings in this book.

My thanks and gratitude to Roger Walsh, Stanley Krippner, and especially, Stan Grof, who saw my drawings and used them in their work and whose early belief in me encouraged my efforts to get this book into a publishable format. To Tanya Wilkinson, my grateful thanks for her contribution to this book, which gave me another lens through which to view and appreciate these drawings.

To my children, Mitchell and Stephanie, who endured so much and understood so little of those painful years, my deepest love and empathy for your own struggles; may this book ultimately shed some light and aid in your understanding of those years.

To my good friend and colleague, Maryjane Dunstan, whose belief in me consistently inspired me through revision after revision, and whose keen intelligence and no-nonsense, 'book-savvy' feedback aided me immeasurably in shaping this material, my heartfelt gratitude and thanks.

To my friend, Joyce Post, whose invaluable expert assistance in transmitting and retrieving e-mail attachments and in mentoring my wanderings through the mysterious mazes of my computer enabled the completion of this book, my abundant thanks.

And finally, my grateful thanks and appreciation to: Rick Doblin at MAPS, my publisher, whose enthusiasm for the manuscript and care for this project assured me that I had placed this material in the most perfect of hands; Tim Butcher, whose exquisite vision and exhaustive work faithfully and brilliantly scanned my drawings for this book; Maggie Hall, my editor, whose relaxed, consistent good-humor and careful, intelligent editing was invaluable in the publication of this book.

– Sherana Harriette Frances

Author's Note:

As is the custom in the Greek Orthodox culture into which I was born, my given name, Harriette (translated from the Greek, Χαρικλεια), was selected by my Godparents and not revealed to my parents until it was bestowed upon me at my christening. It is the name by which I was known at the time of the experiences related in this book and at the time I met (some years later) Stan Grof and Tanya Wilkinson. Although this name was always an uncomfortable fit, it was not until well after my parents' deaths that I felt removed enough from the echoes of the old traditions to freely use my chosen name.

Sherana Harriette Frances.

CONTENTS

INTRODUCTION
by Stanislav Grof, M.D.

A SERENDIPITOUS DISCOVERY by an unknown Swiss chemist in the middle of WW II initiated what many consider to be the golden era of consciousness research. In 1943, Dr. Albert Hofmann, working in the laboratories of the Sandoz pharmaceutical company in Basel, accidentally intoxicated himself and discovered the powerful psychedelic effects of diethylamide of lysergic acid, a substance that would later become world-renown as LSD-25. After the publication of the first clinical paper on LSD by Walter A. Stoll in the late 1940s, Albert Hofmann's discovery of the psychedelic effects of LSD became practically an overnight sensation in the world of science. Never before had a single substance held so much promise in such a wide variety of fields of interest.

For neuropharmacologists and neurophysiologists, the discovery of LSD meant the beginning of a golden era of research that could solve many puzzles concerning the intricate biochemical interactions underlying the functioning of the brain.

Experimental psychiatrists saw this substance as a unique means for creating a laboratory model for naturally occurring psychoses, particularly schizophrenia. They hoped that it could provide unparalleled insights into the nature of these mysterious disorders and open new avenues for their treatment.

Early experiments with LSD revealed its unique potential as a powerful tool offering the possibility of deepening and accelerating the psychotherapeutic process, as well as extending the range of applicability of psychotherapy to categories of patients that previously had been difficult to reach such as alcoholics, narcotic drug addicts, and criminal recidivists.

Particularly valuable and promising were the early efforts to use LSD psychotherapy with terminal cancer patients. These studies showed that LSD was able to relieve severe pain, often even in those patients who had not responded to medication with narcotics. In a large percentage of these patients, it was also possible to alleviate or even eliminate the fear of death, increase the quality of their life during the remaining days, and positively transform the experience of dying.

LSD was also highly recommended as a unique teaching device that would make it possible for clinical psychiatrists and psychologists to spend a few hours in the world of their patients. As a result of this experience they could understand them better, be able to communicate with them more effectively, and improve their ability to help them.

For the historians and critics of art, the LSD experiments provided extraordinary new insights into the psychology and psychopathology of art, particularly the paintings and sculptures of native cultures and various modern movements, such as surrealism, fantastic realism, cubism, expressionism, and abstractionism.

The spiritual experiences frequently observed in LSD sessions offered a radically new understanding of a wide variety of phenomena from the world of religion, including shamanism, the rites of passage, the ancient mysteries of death and rebirth, the Eastern spiritual philosophies, and the mystical traditions of the world.

LSD research seemed to be well on its way to fulfilling all of the above promises and expectations when it was suddenly interrupted by unsupervised mass experimentation of the young generation and the ensuing repressive measures of a legal, administrative, and political nature. At present, the future of psychedelics as clinical and research tools does not look very bright, in spite of the fact that a few researchers have been granted permission to resume some limited experimentation with these substances. However, the two decades during which this research flourished in many countries of the world amassed revolutionary new information about the psyche that is of lasting value. It is, therefore, important to preserve as many documents of these pioneering efforts as possible.

I do not know of any single document illustrating the extraordinary healing and transformative potential of psychedelics in a way that matches in its importance this book by Harriette Frances and the unique illustrations that accompany it.

There are many reasons why it stands in a category of its own. The author is a woman of extraordinary intelligence and capacity for psychological insight. However, she began her journey of self-exploration without any specific intellectual knowledge in the areas of Jungian psychology, mythology, comparative religion, and anthropology. For this reason, there can not be any doubt that the astonishing images that erupted from the depth of her psyche are genuine products of her unconscious.

Although the immediate impulse for the opening of her individual and collective unconscious was her psychedelic session at Menlo Park in the early 1960s, the treasure trove of her psyche remained open and available to her during the subsequent years of her work with hypnosis and drug-free psychotherapy. This shows that a single psychedelic experience can initiate an ongoing, possibly lifelong, process of self-exploration. During her ongoing adventure of self-discovery that has extended over a period of several decades, Harriette Frances has brought convincing evidence that the human psyche reaches far beyond the narrow limits outlined by traditional psychology and psychiatry.

She underwent a powerful process of psychospiritual death and rebirth that included the elements of her own trauma of birth and prenatal existence. Her journey took her even farther back, to what seems to be her ancestral and possibly karmic past, as she herself suggested. The magnificent imagery involving the bull certainly brings to mind the importance that this animal played in the mythology, spiritual and ritual life, and even everyday existence in the Minoan culture in Crete, the island of her origin. We can think here of Europa carried to Crete by Zeus in the form of a giant white bull, the story of the Minotaur and the labyrinth, and the Minoan ritual gymnastic games involving adolescents and bulls.

But the excursions that Harriette Frances took to the depth of her psyche and to the remote past were not the goal in and of themselves. It was in these realms where she found the deep roots of some problems that plagued her in her personal life. Bringing this material into consciousness and integrating it helped her to reach a new balance between the feminine and masculine elements in her psyche, accept the death of her father, and come to terms with the problems in her marriage and in her relationships with men. Her healing has come from levels that are beyond the reach of traditional therapy. There is little doubt that the probing of the psyche to this depth was made possible by her experiences of nonordinary states of consciousness.

Another reason why Harriette Frances' book is such a unique psychological document is her extraordinary capacity to find artistic expression for visionary experiences. Astonishing visual richness is a very characteristic feature of the experiences with LSD, psilocybin, mescaline, and other psychedelics. People who have experimented with these substances often talk about 'orgies of vision,' 'retinal circus,' or 'optical cornucopia'. However, equally frequent are complaints about the inability to capture these visions artistically and bring them back to others. Harriette Frances did not let herself be discouraged by the technical difficulties associated with this task. She was able to create some of the best visionary art I know about anywhere in the world. Her ability to find artistic expression for the images from the depth of her psyche is truly extraordinary!

Harriette Frances' healing journey was a long one and it took her into areas that are not recognized and appreciated by Western academic science. And yet that was where the most powerful healing occurred. I hope this will serve as an important incentive for mainstream therapists to widen their horizons and extend their cartography of the psyche to include these realms. At present, the possibility of reliving birth episodes from embryonic life, obtaining accurate information from the collective unconscious, experiencing archetypal realities, and reliving karmic memories appears to be too fantastic to be believable for an average professional.

Yet those of us who had the chance to work with psychedelics and other powerful experiential forms of psychotherapy, and were willing to radically change our theoretical understanding of the psyche and practical strategy of therapy, were able to see and appreciate the enormous therapeutic potential of non-ordinary states of consciousness. The legal and administrative sanctions against psychedelics did not deter lay experimentation, but they terminated all legitimate scientific research of these substances. For those of us who had the privilege to explore the extraordinary potential of psychedelics, this was a tragic loss for psychiatry, psychology, and psychotherapy. We felt that these unfortunate developments wasted what was probably the single most important opportunity in the history of these disciplines.

We can only guess what would have happened had the legislation been more reasonable and had Harriette Frances been able to continue her therapy and self-exploration in supervised psychedelic sessions. It would most likely have accelerated her healing process and taken her to many additional adventures within her own psyche. Those of us who have the privilege to share the artistic treasures in her present book can only fantasize what the images from those excursions would have looked like. And, of course, we hope that her inner journey will continue in the future and that she will share it with us in the same way that she has her extraordinary explorations in the past.

– Stanislav Grof, M. D., Mill Valley, California

PROLOGUE: CAULDRON OF REGENERATION:
Psychological Transformation in the Drawings of Harriette Frances
by Tanya Wilkinson, Ph.D.

HARRIETTE FRANCES journeyed into her unconscious with the help of a hallucinogenic drug. She descended into an underworld of dismemberment and regeneration. Her descents were undertaken because she "badly wanted access to the secret part of myself". Her drawings of these journeys function for her still as "unfailing guides, healers, prophets and teachers". What was the situation in Frances' life that called for guidance, healing and instruction?

Her personal struggle in 1963 reflected a destructive split between her rigid gender role, that of the traditional wife and mother, and the talents and preferences of her inner self, an artist. Patriarchal divisions ran through Frances' life, fracturing career, creativity, relationships and self, creating as she has said, "a dichotomy... a duality and ultimately a duplicity" while she longed to be whole. These drawings portray one woman's embodiment of a split in the self and her symbolic, yet visceral bridging of that split. Her journey also maps the separation in Western patriarchal culture between the conscious, upper world realm of rational, conventional expectations and the culturally denied underworld of the unconscious, a cauldron of mysteries and non-rational experience.

Frances' descent proved fruitful and, after many struggles to integrate its revelations, she changed her life. Many women did not and do not return from the underworld. It may be that Frances' profound portrayal of descent and return can provide a light of guidance and faith, a sense of the inner resources of transformation available even to those who feel, as Frances did in 1963, utterly trapped by internal and external social constraints.

The Unconscious as a Storehouse of Transformative Images

What are these inner resources of transformation? Jung's conceptualization of the unconscious provides us with a way of understanding the psychological, emotional and spiritual experience portrayed in Frances' drawings. In general the purpose of the unconscious is compensatory. Normal consciousness in the well-adapted Western individual is necessarily one-sided, dominated by an ego concerned with relating effectively to cultural norms and conventional truth, just as Frances' conscious view of her conflict was dominated by her need to fit in as a "good woman". Conventional truth in the West is heavily masculinized, intellectualized, positivistic and materialistic. Consequently much of human experience that is mysterious, without boundaries, feminine, emotional, spiritual, creative and raw lives in the unconscious, usually in an undifferentiated state. The compensatory purpose of the unconscious is to balance and regenerate consciousness by communicating denied aspects of the self and the world to the dominant, culture-identified ego. (I use ego here in the way that Jung used it—to indicate those aspects of the self that are consciously acknowledged by the individual.) Thus the unconscious functions as a storehouse of forgotten resources which it communicates through the medium of symbolic dialogue.

The forms of symbolic communication between conscious and unconscious aspects of the self are myriad. Images and narratives encountered in dreams, trance states (however induced) and states of reverie, such as daydream, are the most obvious symbolic products of the unconscious. Unconscious material is also woven throughout the warp of everyday life. The experience of inexplicable revulsion and attraction, gripping moods and body states that appear to have little or no basis in external events, compulsive behaviors, seemingly random thought streams, intense responses to people—any or all such experiences may spring from the unconscious. Frances' conscious loyalty to the gender role expectations of her community and her husband made it nearly impossible for her to validate any of the daily communications of the unconscious, although they caused her great discomfort, a feeling of being subject to "demonic intruders". Nonetheless, when the drug LSD opened a gateway to the unconscious, within the safe container of the research project, an archetypal experience of dismemberment, insight and rebirth was readily accessible, the forgotten resources were tapped.

The Necessity of the Container

What conditions are necessary to achieve access to such unconscious resources of transformation? The reality of the psyche is multifaceted and contradictory even in the absence of a major conflict like the one tearing Frances apart at the time of her LSD experience. Although I have used the notion of the storehouse to convey a sense of the resources of the unconscious, it is perhaps too orderly an image. Personal and transpersonal aspects of the unconscious are woven together (it might be more viscerally correct to say mashed together) and do not become differentiated until they are brought to awareness. Repressed pathogens intersect with unrealized spiritual potentials in ways that can be profoundly confusing and sometimes dangerous. So, the experience of accessing the unconscious is not like opening an ordered storehouse and selecting a transformative resource but rather like plunging into a swirling cauldron. Successful access to the transformative power of the unconscious requires an adequate container; the cauldron must have sturdy sides to withstand the chaos of regeneration.

The concept of the container, as used here, springs from the practice of depth psychotherapy. Various names are used in that practice—container, temenos, holding function, frame—to denote a bounded, some would say sacred, space within the therapeutic relationship, a space which is needed to facilitate the symbolic dialogue. The container holds the rich chaos of conscious and unconscious experience, allows a multitude of fragmentary images to be sorted out and deeply felt, to interrelate and be held in consciousness. The container provides a framework for the bridging of split worlds, for the recognition of revolutionary insights which the socially conditioned ego might otherwise avoid.

The ego's task in the process of making such a container is not its usual one of analysis, judgment, categorization and control. Instead the ego shifts, using a more observing, empathetic, aesthetic and perhaps feminine stance which allows all stories to be told, to complement one another, until a picture of the personal myth is built up. This shift in ego stance must be actively supported by the nature of the relationships that nurture the container. The need to actively build and nurture such a container, whether in therapy or out, is particularly pressing for an individual who has been conditioned to distrust inner perceptions in favor of social expectations. The careful, thoughtful process provided by the researchers and their validation of the importance of Frances' experience created a sacred space for her initial contact with the transformative, archetypal energies depicted in her drawings. Eventually the drawing process itself provided a container for cyclical journeys of descent and renewal.

    – Tanya Wilkinson, Ph.D., Professor of Psychology and core Faculty Member at the California Institute of Integral Studies, San Francisco, California, and licensed psychotherapist in private practice. Author; *Medea's Folly*, and *Persephone Returns*.

Drawing It Out: Befriending the Unconscious

Sherana Harriette Frances

SECTION ONE: The Descent
The Trip Begins...

A HOUSEWIFE IN MENLO PARK found "total love" in a drug-filled chalice; a technical book editor in Oakland had his life so totally reshaped by a "dream drug" that he fired his psychiatrist; artists, writers, bankers, students, educators – all kinds of people in the Bay Area were finding "instant Zen" and "psychiatry in a bottle"– and they were reportedly waking up to "permanently higher levels of awareness and deeper levels of self-understanding". All this from an extraordinary invisible, tasteless, odorless speck of chemical weighing 1/200,000ths of an ounce, capable of inducing staggering visions and mystical experiences beyond the ordinary mind — all this from a speck of LSD-25.

From my home in the San Joaquin Valley of California, I read with mounting excitement these remarkable stories, reported under sensational headline banners in the San Francisco papers and in magazines to which I subscribed. All these stories hinted at spectacular 'cures' for a variety of disorders with this miracle drug. For me, all this meant it was a time of hope, pregnant with possibilities that I wanted to explore; it was a time when I, too, could "go out of my mind to come to my senses". It was 1963... and for me, the times, they were "a-changing".

...

In the spring of 1963, while my husband was at work and my two kids were in school, I backed my car out of the garage and headed west from my home in the San Joaquin Valley. In the spacious trunk I had carefully packed three items—an overnight bag along with two of my recent paintings, although this time I was not en route to deliver them to a distant gallery. This time, I was heading for Menlo Park, and ultimately, for a far more remote destination—to an unimaginable space where I was about to join the scores of "middle and upper class intelligentsia" flocking from the "suberbohemia" of the San Francisco Bay Area (as one reporter put it) for the trip of a lifetime. It was a trip from which I never, in a true sense, returned home. Nothing was ever the same after my visit to the immense worlds opened up by a speck of chemical, diethylamide of d-lysergic acid, commonly referred to as LSD-25.

I had initially made contact by telephone with the International Foundation for Advanced Study in Menlo Park, California, excited by the daily reports of the seemingly instant levels of awareness and serenity reached by those who had access to this "dream drug". It was there that these experiments were taking place, and my first interview was scheduled for the fall of 1962. For several months following my first appointment, I made frequent visits to the Foundation for a series of preparations before the controlled experience with LSD would take place. I was a voluntary participant, with my husband's reluctant approval, in the Foundation's program of research in experimental therapy with the drug, LSD, and I had been looking forward to the actual experience after what had seemed like interminable months of interviews, tests and evaluations by the Foundation's staff.

With this chemical assistance, I was sure I would be able to explore the hidden recesses and outer boundaries of my mind. There, I hoped, I would find answers to the troubling and fearful questions of my life. After all, these were the "dream drugs" sensationalized in the daily papers; these were the agents that produced "revelations on the head of a pin"—that had reshaped a man's life, that had let everyone, from housewives to movie stars, in on the secrets of "man's fate, man's being, man's involvement with his fellows and with the universe—questions which have confronted man for thousands of years". Surely there was room here for a woman's fate, a woman's being, and my questions about my own place in the larger picture. Without question, these amazing testimonies on a daily basis seduced me, and I had high hopes for the outcome of my own journey.

It was in this frame of mind that I climbed the stairs to the second floor of the modest building housing the International Foundation for Advanced Study, at the time of my first appointment in 1962. I was immediately assailed by the subtle yet distinctive odor that I later came to associate with the Foundation. It was a "hospital" kind of smell, permeating the hallway and greeting me on each of my many visits over the ensuing months. I later identified it as the slight but discernible odor of "carbogen", a mixture of 70% carbon dioxide and 30% oxygen-this mixture was administered as an inhalant to the participants in the research program, for periods of approximately six weeks before the ingestion of LSD, as "simulation training" for the feeling of surrender to an altered state.

On my first visit, I nervously thumbed through the assorted magazines in the waiting room, but the vague hospital smell sent my anxiety level soaring. I soon gave up the pretense of reading, and instead began to dwell on the terrible impasse in my troubled marriage, a "ménage a trois" in a combat of such deadly proportions that it had precipitated my several suicide attempts. This huge burden of guilt and depression was affecting the entire family, pushing us into our separate, unhappy corners. My bewildered children were asking silent questions with their eyes. And yet, I would not, could not give up this intruder in our marriage, this unwelcome "third party" with whom I insisted on consorting, with whom I had gone to bed ever since I could remember, and whom my husband called a "demon". I didn't know how to separate myself from this demon, even though it seemed to be destroying us all; because this demon was, in fact, my passion for art and my lifelong dream of following wherever it would lead me. If LSD could dissolve the barriers between my conscious and unconscious mind, I would be able to see those deeper areas that housed not only my dream but this demon—and maybe then I would understand how this creative force that sustained my life could also be the same force that was destroying it.

When the door to one of the offices opened, I looked up expectantly. Just a few moments more, a staff member told me, and then I would be ushered in. I spent those moments reviewing the literature that outlined the purposes behind the research and experiments with hallucinogenic drugs.

It seemed that the Foundation's program was partly educational, partly mystical, partly scientific, partly philosophical and partly medical. Through the volumes of statistics they were compiling, they hoped to find a correlation between the LSD experience and other extraordinary, or "altered states", such as hypnosis, transcendental experiences, dreams, and the phenomenon of religious conversion.

They had certainly carved out an ambitious program, but those inquiries held mild interest for me. My concerns were more personal. My interest had to do with their inquiries into whether or not the drug experience was, in essential ways, similar to the creative process—because this was the very process that was wreaking havoc in my marriage and my life—and had brought me to the Foundation in search of answers.

From all the accounts in the papers and all I had read in the literature of the Foundation, the concept behind their program seemed to be that an individual could have one experience so vitally profound that all following experience would become a continuous process of consciousness-expansion and growth. Who wouldn't be intrigued by this concept! It is no wonder these strange hallucinatory drugs appealed even to those who administered them, and to scientists who, in order to study severe mental illness, "risked insanity to cure insanity", as one reporter suggested.

I imagined my life changing in an instant, each day opening to serenity, an end to conflict and confusion. With the turn of a chemical key, the lights would go on in all the dark rooms of my mind—I would find the demon, slay it, and put an end to its passionate and unrelenting embrace of my life. My husband viewed this passion of mine as a stubborn, wilful and selfish indulgence, one which relegated the concerns of our domestic life to a secondary status; I, on the other hand, did not view it as a choice but a necessity, as vital to me as breathing. But, since I had not been able to reconcile what seemed like my two separate identities, constantly at war, one of them had to go. One of them, finally, had to die. And the weight of evidence seemed to point to the driving force of my life. I had seen, in the depth of my husband's pain and in the urgency of my own, that it was time to kill that which was surely killing us, and thereby enter into the peaceful kingdom that had, so far, eluded us.

I had no guides or role models, not in my immigrant parents from the isle of Crete, nor in our Greek community, as to how to successfully balance both, since my culture valued domesticity as a higher priority over "careers" for women. Further, and more damaging, I had privately accepted my husband's view of me as a driven, selfish woman whose "demon" was responsible for all the unhappiness, confusion, desperation and depression that preyed upon our marriage.

And so, in the seventeenth year of a desperate marriage, of daily confrontation between the demands of our household and the demands of my "demon," of growing confusion and painful distress in the eyes of my children, I pinned my hopes on LSD. I would, like the others I had read about, go "out of my mind to come to my senses". I would be one of the elite to find my way out of chaos by entering it.

Once again, the door opened, and I was ushered into the comfortable office of the Medical Director for my first interview. Dr. Charles Savage, the Medical Director, introduced me to

Dr. John Sherwood, who joined in the ensuing interview, and to Myron Stolaroff (the author of *The Secret Chief*), who was then president of their Board of Directors. Further introductions were made to some of the friendly staff and research analysts who would be conducting future interviews. A series of appointments followed in which psychological and psychiatric evaluations and tests were administered, designed to assess values, personality and beliefs. Among these, I remember especially the Minnesota Multiphasic Personality Inventory (MMPI), a frustrating and cleverly posed series of questions to which, as I recall, only "yes" or "no" answers were permitted, shaded with a pencil in the appropriate circles on the endless pages. My instinctive answers were usually "yes, but…" and "no, only when…", averaging out as "sometimes"–and it took a considerable and aggravating time to find the answer closest to my own truth. One of the tests I did like was something called the "T.A.T.", or "Thematic Apperception Test", in which I was asked to supply the story behind the incomplete images on a series of cards – and I also favored the Rorschach test, in which abstract blobs appeared at times beautiful and at times sinister. I recall, also, a value-sorting test, where I stacked squares of paper in the order of importance of the information contained, representing an assigned value. All these tests were designed to help the staff evaluate our individual perceptions, but I always felt apprehensive, that my own truthful answers were on trial as "right" or "wrong".

Each week there were more interviews eliciting autobiographical material, as well as extensive reading lists, more value-sorting tests, more interviews, and the dreaded MMPI test, which surfaced at spaced intervals over the ensuing weeks. There were, throughout these weeks, intense periods of stating and restating the questions that brought me to the Foundation, in both written and oral form, designed to help me examine and clarify these concerns. Each week I was getting closer to the day when I would be ready, both in the Foundation's estimation and my own, for my date with LSD.

For each of the six weeks prior to the actual LSD experience, I was given carbogen, that mixture with the now familiar smell, which I inhaled through a face-mask similar to hospital ether masks, until I became accustomed to the feeling of an altered state and learned to "let go". There was an initial anxiety as the mask enveloped my face, plunging me into utter darkness as I lost consciousness. Over the weeks, however, it became a familiar experience; I knew the darkness would shift, almost immediately, to become illuminated with vividly colored shapes and dream-like forms. These experiences were intensely real, involving activity in my physical body as well as in my mind. I remember "waking up" from one of those sessions, my body crawling on the floor and my arms tightly gripped around the legs of one of the research staffers. Sometimes I remembered "where I went" and other times remembered only the darkness; sometimes I moaned, or cried or laughed.

The time came when all of us were satisfied that I was sufficiently prepared, and my date with LSD was finally scheduled. It was to be on a March morning in 1963.

I was on my way to the fateful meeting, with my two paintings and an overnight bag. I drove to the Foundation and climbed the stairs, each step with a rising excitement, in anticipation of the leap into hidden and unexplored territory I was about to take. Just as an artist feels when confronting an empty canvas, I was about to jump into the unknown. At 8:00 a.m., I was led into a quiet, beautifully furnished room with a serene golden Buddha at one end; a small portrait of Christ was elsewhere in the room. I propped up my two paintings, and the photos of my family, so I could see them from the comfortable sofa where I had settled down. At 8:36 a.m., I was given the premeasured dose of LSD; the "Grand Canyon Suite" and other music of my choice was on my headphones. My guides, Mary A. Hughes (a medical doctor) and Bob Leihy (then a research analyst), settled in for the duration of my journey. They were there to provide guidance and emotional support, as needed, and otherwise did not intrude on my experience. Throughout the day they stayed with me, and towards evening another guide accompanied me to a nearby motel, to monitor and support me as the effects of the drug waned and eventually wore off, in the late hours of that night.

The following morning, I arose early. Deep inside, I felt both a deep exhaustion and a keen agitation. I arrived at the Foundation for a short follow-up interview and assessment of my experience, and I remember apologizing because I had cried so much. They asked me to send a written report of what I had experienced, whatever I thought was significant to me. And then I went home. In the car with me were my two paintings—plus a cargo of kaleidoscopic images from the shattered reality in my mind.

I had gone into this experience knowing I had to find answers to the urgent questions of my life, finally and forever. And certainly I had clarified, in my own mind, that either I had to accept and live with this despair—or die from it. So what I wanted, essentially, from this experience with LSD, was to save my life—what I found in that experience was, in essence, my "death", the total disintegration of my sense of self, my sense of reality—and my sense of who or what it is that runs this awesome show.

This had been called a "dream drug"—and I had found terrifying nightmares. It had been touted as the doorway to ecstatic life—and I had been wandering in the graveyards of death. That it was capable of "mind-quakes" was more than abundantly true. I had been shaken down to my bones, my core turned inside out. I was not the same woman driving home. Nor could I guess at the nature of the resynthesis, and its drastic consequences that stretched ahead.

RE-ENTRY

The Foundation's interest in the participants didn't end with the drug experience and the morning-after interview. For approximately six months following the experience, I went back for additional interviews, personality inventories, tests, reports and evaluations, conducted by various researchers. Among those interviewing me were Dr. Robert Mogar, then Assistant Professor of Psychology at San Francisco State University and Director of Research at the Foundation; and James Fadiman, then a Ph.D. candidate at Stanford and research associate at the Foundation. The data collected allowed researchers to analyze what changes an individual underwent following a psychedelic experience. The changes in which they were interested were in three main dimensions: values and beliefs, personality, and actual behavior in significant life areas.

According to Dr. Robert Mogar, this data pointed to the recurrence of some themes— for example, some form of "death and rebirth", a sense of "self as creator", and an experience of "unity with all life". Mogar suggested that the significance of such themes, growing out of the data collected, might serve as an important link to dreams and archetypal images. This was heady stuff indeed, but that was not something I knew about at the time of my own experience; not until many years later did I realize the significance of my own contribution to this data.

As a visual artist, I found words to be totally inadequate to describe the experience. I was immensely frustrated in my many attempts to put that experience into words, into the report that the Foundation had requested. Added to that was the fact that in the very early 1960s, when my experience took place, there was no vocabulary for that kind of hallucinatory journey; even the word "psychedelic" was not yet in popular usage. When I finally mailed in a short written report to the Foundation, I felt I had missed the mark by a mile, and then some. The words were not on the same plane as the images.

The "incompleteness" of that report, the sense of unfinished business, was with me day and night, images and sensations from the experience disturbing my sleep. Each day I was growing more inwardly agitated; the chemical key had unlocked, not answers, but a Pandora's Box full of buzzing questions. There were bizarre and awesome worlds, still locked inside me, totally out of kilter with my everyday reality; and I couldn't verbalize it to anyone. My husband, a conservative man who lived in the literal world, could not appreciate the visionary dimensions of my experience; he was not insensitive to my agitation but since any attempted discussion about the experience led to more difficulties, he ultimately stopped asking questions, unable to take on my distress in addition to his own. I knew, however, he was hoping that the demon we had coped with for so long was finally put to rest, or at the very least, would take a back seat in our lives, now that the experience was over. Both of us were keenly aware of the unspoken questions of our children and both of us hoped, for all our sakes, that somehow we could salvage what was left of our marriage, since the alternative was too painful to contemplate.

And so I lived with the imbalance the LSD experience had brought to my life. In my circle of friends, none of the other young wives or mothers had been crazy enough to seek the kind of experience I had sought. None, so far as I knew, had been curious enough and desperate enough, as I had been, to want to go out of their minds to find meaning and purpose in their lives. There was only one person who would understand, because he, too, had been through the experience. He was an art instructor at a local school and I had been drawn to his boldly conceived canvasses, shown in regional galleries, long before I met him. He subsequently became my special friend and studio-mate, sharing a modest studio on the outskirts of town where we offered occasional classes in painting and life-drawing and where I felt at home with the kindred spirits who hung around to do and "talk art".

For the first time in my life I had found a true soul mate, to whom there was no need to explain the profound need, importance and inevitability of art in my life. Soon we each became the keeper of the other's dreams and confidences and, ultimately, our mutually unfulfilled lives fueled a desperate intimacy, adding to the emotional confusion in which I lived. But shortly after my experience with LSD, he moved out of our studio for a more lucrative teaching job at a distant college, taking with him his darkly seductive canvasses, along with the music and poetry of my life. He had filled a huge void, providing the ballast I had needed. Though I longed for the comfort of his understanding, the pain of his departure had spilled over to seriously affect my already precarious marriage; it would have been folly to attempt reconnection with him. And so I remained, essentially, quite alone with the experience, suspended somewhere between illusion and reality, pregnant with visions of a world that nothing on this earth had prepared me for.

I knew the Foundation deserved a better description of my experience than the report I had sent; but still I was stymied for words. How could I describe the worlds in which, for a space of unreal time, my eyes had seen the visible behind the invisible, the vibrating kaleidoscopic dance beneath it all? I could tell them that the world of my LSD experience was dark and radiant, cold and hot, fearful and ecstatic, hellish and heavenly. But these were only everyday words and far too poor to accurately describe a place where colors were sounds and sounds were colors, where music danced, becoming strands of colored energy in the air—a place where all my senses were insanely transposed, where the function of my ear became the function of my eye; where images became texture and texture became sound; where I became part of the geometrically patterned spiraling dance; where I plunged into the dark and freezing bone yards of my own death, watched the strange disintegration of my own body; where shimmering strands repaired it; and where hieroglyphics danced on the tip of a body where its head should have been.

Nowhere in all the vocabulary I had at my command would I ever find the words for a world where I was rescued from the graveyards through an opening of birds and pulled into a burnt-sienna/yellow ochre landscape… where I experienced an elongated rib-cage stretching out of my body in a desert of vibrating sand… where my flesh was restored by a bird whose flaming wings covered the sky… where I walked past skeletal fish on scorching sands… where I rested on a skeletal cross and watched a dance of prisms and circles… where my husband's face became a boulder that was crushing me with its weight… where menacing shapes flew from my paintings to hang over my body… and where I walked through corridors of canvas, warding off a fatal weight of tears.

When I swam with the fishes, talked with a peacock, and ultimately, perched on the Corinthian column of my ancestors, embracing a dazzling universe, surrounded by a radiance of birds,—what words could I use for a report to the Foundation? And, were I to find them, what could I possibly say it meant?

DRAWING IT OUT.

One night, tip-toeing so as not to awaken my husband, I went to my desk and turned on the small tensor lamp. My heart was pounding and subtle tremors shook me from deep inside as I reached for my drawing tablet. This inner trembling was familiar to me; I had often experienced it when I was on the verge of a breakthrough during a painting impasse at the studio. Sitting at my desk, I tried to "re-view" my experience with LSD. At the Foundation, thousands of images had flown in the space between two beats of my heart, impossible to capture now. Closing my eyes and visualizing the room with the golden Buddha, I let myself drift into the luminous geometry of that extraordinary space.

In this relaxed but intently focused state, I was able to hold for moments at a time those images that significantly described the most pertinent elements of my journey. And when my mind was still enough and my hand steady enough, I turned to my tablet and started to draw. In this deeply quiet, focused state resembling a trance, I began making marks suggesting, but never capturing, the radiant, kaleidoscopic dancing elements, the vibrating particles in space, and the paradoxically illumined darkness of the altered reality in which I had wandered in search of my "demon". With a fine-tipped pen, in black ink on white paper, I began drawing out the essential meaning of my extraordinary journey, line by slow, meditative line. Each mark seemed to take me back in time, to a place where my internal agitation lived side by side with an inexplicable serenity; and when I finally looked up from my drawing tablet, several long quiet hours had passed. I still had not emptied myself of the visions, but now I had one drawing, tracing a part of my experience and releasing me from part of its burden. I had found the right language for this experience at last.

Sandwiched into my "real" life in the weeks that followed was the other reality, now visible on paper in the drawing stack that was growing daily. My memory of that time short-changes me, dropping most activity except the activity of my hand moving across paper. It was releasing me from the inner discomfort that had been a constant companion since my return from the Foundation, but it was also consuming whole days of my time. Each drawing itself took hours, at times well over a half day to complete, during which I truly had no conception of the passing time. I know I attended to household necessities, family concerns, routine chores, but the most urgent thing on my mind seemed to be getting to the drawings, through which the LSD experience was, in a sense, regurgitated. Each finished drawing afforded me one more increment of relief from the internal turmoil. I drew slowly; my mind, in a meditative state, directing the delicate, spidery circling and crawling of lines across the page, forming paradoxically raw and powerful images.

Six weeks and eighteen drawings later, I felt sufficiently emptied. I now had a belated, but more accurate, description of my LSD experience. This was the series of drawings I submitted to the Foundation. (See Series 1, Drawings 1 through 18.)

I had not done this type of drawing before, neither as a professional exhibiting artist nor in my personal sketchbooks, and it is not my usual style of drawing now. It had surfaced only as a tool which allowed me to "draw out" information that was relevant to me. In this consecutive visual form, it was the first graphic, visual record of the LSD experience that the Foundation's staff had ever seen. I had thought, when I completed these drawings, that I had drawn out only my own personal experience. But from input shared with the Foundation, the information seen in this record was relevant to a great many others who viewed these drawings as a valuable visual reference library to the literature of the unconscious. This input was by professional people eminent in fields ranging from art history to archetypal, Jungian, mythological, psychiatric, shamanic and transpersonal disciplines—and I was humbled by it.

Was there more to be seen in these drawings than simply my own personal journey, my own personal and private hells, my own death, and my own transcendent ecstasy? In their cryptic, coded messages, their symbols and hieroglyphics, could I have drawn out a primitive language, touching on a universal journey and an underlying collective memory?

Somehow, through the medium of my hand, insistent images were drawn from a creative source deeper than I had consciously known, a place hitherto untouched in my output as an artist. If I was not consciously directing my hand, who—or what—was?

Could these drawings have been done, not by me but through me? It was, and still is, a humbling thought.

Drawing 1

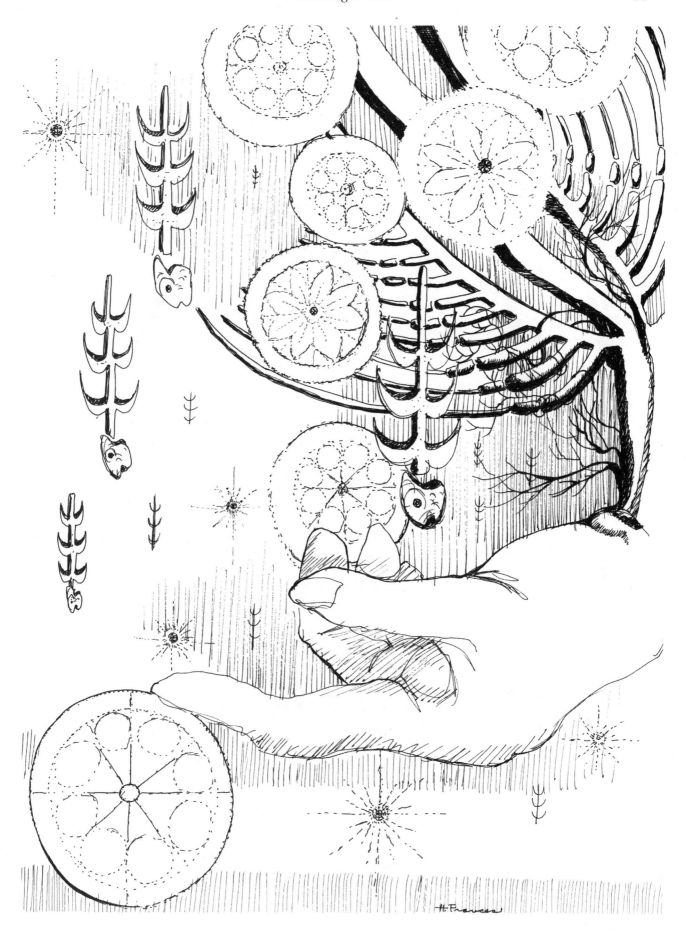

Drawing 2

Drawing 3

Drawing 4

Drawing 5

Drawing 6

Drawing 7

Drawing 8

Drawing 9

Drawing 10

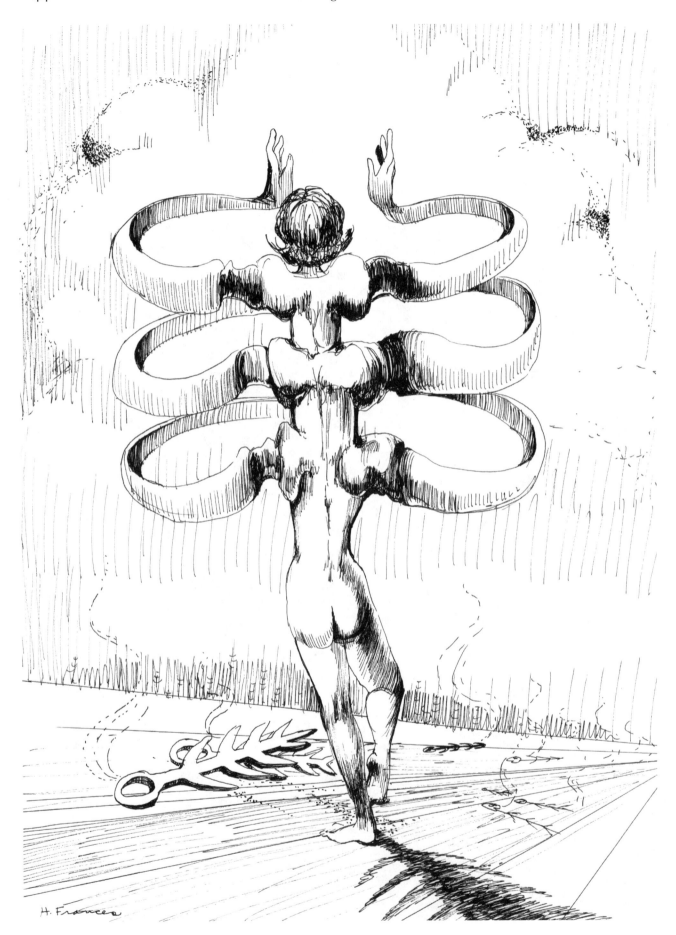

Drawing 11

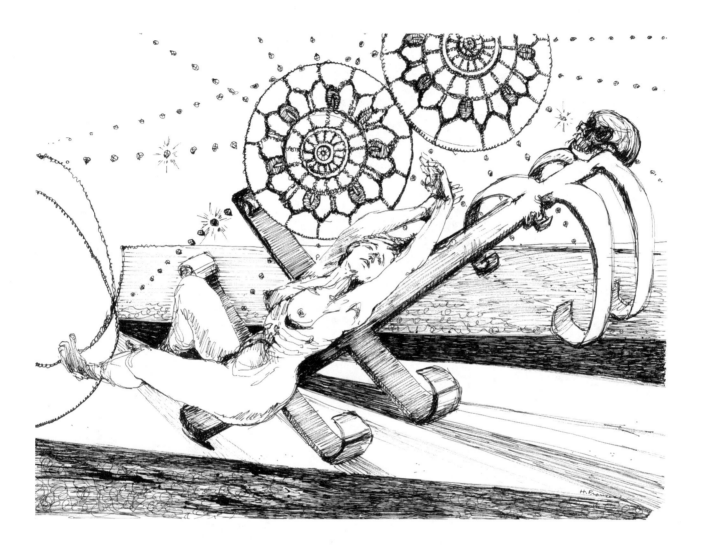

Drawing 12

Drawing 13

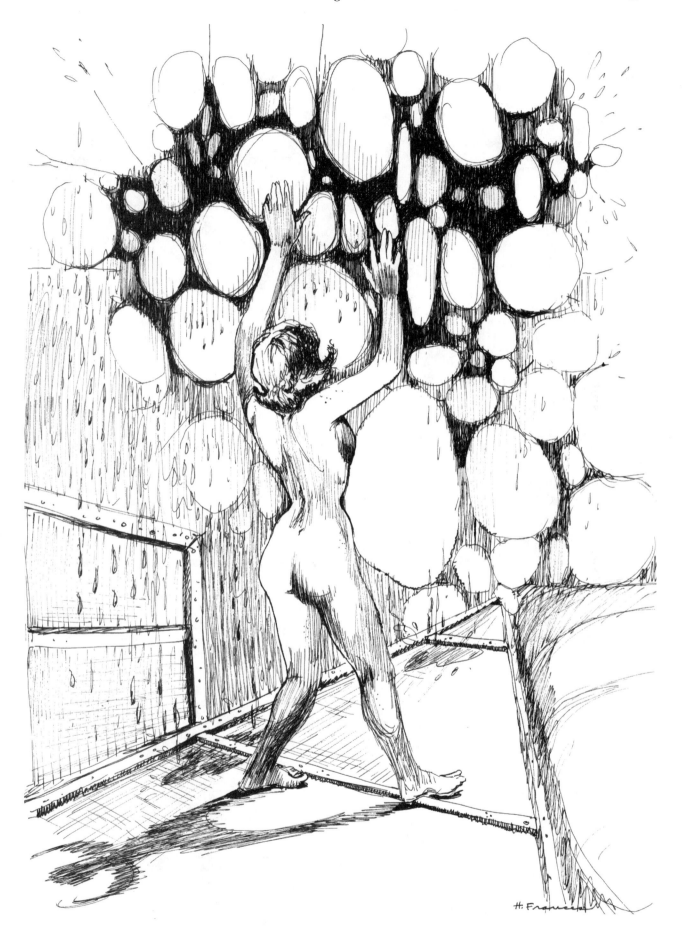

Drawing 14

Drawing 15

Drawing 16

Drawing 17

Drawing 18

SECTION TWO: Drawing Back the Veil

Describing the Indescribable

The dose of LSD, which I had ingested at 8:30 a.m. on that March morning, had, within the hour, begun its work. Behind my eyeshade, the darkness was shifting and changing; the music on my headphones was playing tricks with my mind, thrusting itself into my vision in illumined shapes and dimensional forms, undulating through geometrically patterned and constantly moving space. All the familiar boundaries that gave me my identity were dissolving; I clutched at my clothes to free myself from even their restricting boundaries and joined the swirling, vibrating particles in a golden dance.

By 10:00 a.m., a radiant shimmer of birds joined the expanding light show and then rapidly dissolved into a swirl of multi-colored particles. I felt my body quivering; in an instant the music on my earphones became darkly threatening. A sensation of dread enveloped me as I heard the thunderous roar of a rapid scraping—my eyelashes against the eyeshade. In an ominous departure they became strangely archaic fish-skeletons, floating in a sea of revolving mandalas and prisms of light, radiating alternating waves of heat and cold.

I felt my body melting, coming apart in a burst of particles. A suffocating panic overwhelmed me and I couldn't breathe. I felt myself being pulled into a terrifying darkness, a vortex sucking me down to a place of unearthly cold, into damp and fearful darkness, into the bowels of the earth. In the darkness was an eerie iridescence of bones. I had fallen into the whitely shining bone yards of my own death.

Fear and despair paralyzed me at that level for what seemed an eternity, wandering hopelessly through endless bone yards, skeletons at every turn. Somewhere I could hear the sound of tears, each drop like the thunderous splash of a waterfall. A wail—someone in pain—pounded against my ears. I felt, from some unearthly distance, the touch of someone's hand.

Mary Hughes and Bob Leihy were with me and, seeing my body visibly shaking, Mary asked me if I was cold. In response, my body shivered and she placed a blanket over me. From my prison in the bone yards, I heard a terrible roar, an inhuman, unearthly sound—an anguished cry unlike anything I'd ever heard: it was my own frightened voice, erupting with such terrible force it sent my upper body twisting to the floor, my fists pounding the carpet. My face was wet with uncontrollable tears. Desperately, I clawed at the skeletons and pounded the graveyard floor, crying for help—how had I gotten here—where was the way out?

Bob gently helped me back onto the sofa and asked me to describe where I was. In a frightened voice I told him I was in a graveyard and couldn't find my way out. I was icy cold—I was in the clammy earth, surrounded by skeletons—could they please help? They asked if I thought I could change the scene, suggesting I could imagine the horizon, with the sun warming my chilled body. It was, I believe, the first time I entertained the notion that I, and no one else, had the power to change my own scene. I could be in control of my own reality and I could move on.

Many years later, when I was proficient enough to "read" some of the drawings, I realized that those early drawings clearly show a light-filled "opening" near the top of the page, a way out of the darkness and the bone yards. My drawings, it seems, were telling me—literally, showing me—that I apparently chose to stay paralyzed at that level, rather than risk the way out—even though the way out was there all along. It would have taken, however, more courage than I had then to act on that realization, and more self-awareness than I had at that time to even see it.

From the vantage point of time and more understanding, a few more lessons become apparent in the remarkably instructive drawings from this series, a few of which I will mention here.

In one of the drawings from this series (see Drawing 7) a figure representing me sits pondering a dismembered skeleton with a set of hieroglyphics where the head should be—in the place where thought originates, where what we call our mind is—why had I been looking elsewhere for answers, it seems to say. Hands appear in this series to be passively resting or helplessly gesturing—not being able yet, or not wanting, to "take hold"? And in another,(see Drawing 9) a half-skeletal woman reaches up to a male figure on the horizon, who is extending a helpful hand to her. Here, again, there is helplessness and passive containment in her posture and the posture of her reaching hands—from too much reliance on the male? In this same drawing, the man is poised to pull her out. He is reaching for her from a plateau of the warm earth colors of a painter's palette, "yellow-ochre, burnt sienna"—a rather straightforward depiction of the "salvation" represented by my former studio-mate. Or was it, perhaps, a clear rendering of the relevance of art in my life? And in the drawing where a tiny figure is being crushed under a massive boulder, which bears my husband's face (see Drawing 13), isn't that how I was experiencing the demands of my marriage and my life at that time?

The paintings I had taken with me to the Foundation also became a part of the experience. Looking at them in a drug-induced state was another kind of revelation. My own art works became, at different points in the LSD experience, both threatening and nurturing, things that could kill me as well as things that could save me. In one drawing, I have depicted a corridor of canvas, where tears fall from the colors and shapes of my paintings (see Drawing 14). In the next (Drawing 15), the tears have hardened into icy masses, a cold menace in their hard, jagged and sharp edges but beautiful in their composition. My own paintings overwhelmed me, holding both the promise of fulfillment and the threat of annihilation. They were deceptive surfaces holding my mesmerized attention while they closed in to crush me.

I had never experienced, in quite this visceral way, the unique power of art, or more accurately, its powerful effect in my own life.

My journey, burdened with questions for which I sought answers and illumination in the LSD experience, is depicted in these drawings as culminating in a rapture of ecstasy. My arms are outstretched in the embrace of a serenely radiant universe, in a posture that implies an imminent step into its welcoming arms.

Alas, in my real-life journey, that step was into an abyss of confusion and chaos.

In the Shadow of Tradition.

I had sent in my series of drawings to the Foundation, bringing my report to a more complete conclusion. Now there was nothing to be done but wait for the "new life" to begin, the one I desperately hoped would happen all by itself. It was a hope born, not out of stupidity, but out of a monumental lack of experience as to how a woman was to go about changing anything at all, let alone her life.

My parents, immigrants from the island of Crete, had brought my sister and me up in the old-country ways, clinging to the traditions and people of their homeland. Greek was my first language, which I learned to read and write in the "Greek school" my sister and I attended each day after "American school". Our friends, most of whose parents were also from the island of Crete, observed the same customs and traditions as we did. We had very little contact with the American "foreigners" and, with loving intent, our parents placed definite limitations on their daughters' activities.

I was painfully aware, however, of the sharp contrasts between my life and the lives and freedoms enjoyed by the American youngsters I observed in junior high and high school. For instance, though I was an honor student and a member of the California Scholarship Federation, I never attended any of the meetings, since they were held after school. I was a reporter for our high school paper but turned down any assignments requiring coverage of after-school games or social functions. Instead, I hurried home directly after school as I had been instructed, lest my parents worry at any tardiness, and then spent hours on my homework, my piano lessons, and the wonderful library books in which I found escape and refuge.

As a consequence of our extended trip to visit our relatives in Greece during my grammar school years, I had missed a school term and had been held back in my first term at junior high. However, my diligent study and voracious reading habits soon paid off and I was advanced two grades by the end of my high school year. And so I graduated early, with classmates I did not know, who had gone to proms without me. Though I chafed at my overprotected life, one part of me understood that our parents had placed these restrictions and limitations on their daughters' activities with nothing but loving intent, following the only traditions they knew. And so defiance or rebellion against the wishes of our parents was not even remotely in our plans, nor ever consciously in our minds.

We were destined, then, to live the lives our parents, in their misguided love, wished for us: to become good Greek wives, married as our custom dictated by arrangement, to good

Greek men (preferably with roots in Crete) honoring the traditions of our culture. Careers and choices were reserved for the men; and if somehow a Greek woman aspired to, or had a career of her own, it was assumed that when she married, her career would be put aside.

In those years, marriage was the usual destiny, not only of the Greek women in my culture, but, also, of the American women of my generation. Though I was part of each tradition, the cultural and patriarchal milieu in which my life—and that of most women's—took shape defined not only my duties but my nature as well. My life, therefore, was experienced mostly as acted upon, largely imposed and proscribed by the dictates of men. Having lain in those Procrustean beds, my own growth had been stunted, limiting my reach and distorting my identity.

Though my outer stance was a passive one, I was not in sync with those bi-cultural expectations for women. Inwardly, I had my own visions, my own preferences, and my own dreams for an independent life, but no clue as to how to act on them. My identity as an artist was formed at the age of two, when I discovered the pretty marks crayons made on paper (and sometimes on walls),—and later, in kindergarten, when I discovered paints and saw the wondrous way they dripped down the white paper on the small stand-up easel. When, at age 14, I won a scholarship to the first art school I ever attended, that identity was firmly sealed.

My father, proud of my talent, indulged me in what he assumed was a temporary interest. Three years later, upon my graduation from high school, he enrolled me in a business school so that I could learn a moneymaking skill until I could assume my proper role as somebody's wife. He had not counted on, nor had I dared express, the depth of my passionate interest in pursuing a career in the fine arts. Though I finished at the top of my class in business school and was placed in my first job as a legal secretary, making money was not my goal—making art was.

I had not made an independent decision in my life; but, at age seventeen, I committed my first unorthodox and defiant act in pursuit of my personal dream: I literally dropped to my knees one night to plead with my father for permission to enroll in evening classes at the California School of fine Arts. He and I both understood this to be a daring and desperate gesture, since although I was already working as a legal secretary for a downtown law firm during the day, neither I nor my sister had ever been out at night without a chaperone. If he consented, it would mean my taking public transportation, at night, alone, to get to the art school. Up until this moment, although my sister and I often chafed at the restrictions imposed by our parents, none of their decisions for us had ever been challenged.

I believe my father was deeply shaken, perhaps even frightened, by the intensity of my pleading. I am sure he had never imagined this temporary pastime would become so all consuming. I know he saw, perhaps even felt, my desperation. It was his capitulation on this one immensely important issue that sealed and released, in the most final way, my identity as an artist.

But it was his consent, two years later, to my marriage that signaled, in an unspoken but well-understood way, an end to his support of my dream – and clearly signaled an expectation that now I would put aside my childhood toys and assume my proper responsibilities as wife, helpmate, and mother.

My own expectations were that marriage would take me away from the controlling parameters of my unmarried life, set me free to discover what it was like to be a "grown-up" woman, to be with a man and experience sexual love, and, in some miraculous and unimaginable way, release me to pursue my dream.

And so, each with our own agenda, our own expectations, two almost-strangers were married. John and I had met at the baptism of my cousin's twin girls and danced under our mothers' watchful eyes. Shortly after that, he had joined the Army Air Corps and left for training. The circumstances of our lives were such that we did not see each other for just over a year following our initial meeting, during which time I had continued with my job and my evening art classes. John and I had not seen each other after that initial meeting until he returned. Two months after his return, we were married; until that time, we had never been together without a chaperone. I wasn't sure what love was supposed to feel like but I did think I loved him. Subliminally, I may have felt he was my way out, my ticket to freedom.

Hypnotherapy

That was the background out of which I stepped into the life of a married woman. I was married, as expected, to a good Greek man with traditional values—and expectations I had not anticipated. These required of me an impossible separation: the separation of "the artist" from "the woman". This dichotomy led, one year later, to the office of a psychiatrist—the first of a long string of therapists I would be seeing over the ensuing years. I believe it was in that first year of deep depression, bordering on the catatonic, that the "demon" was driven underground, from where it directed the destructive scenarios played out in our marriage. These warring forces formed the dilemma that had sent me to the Foundation, in a search for answers from LSD.

And now, after that incredible journey, where was the clarity of direction that I had hoped would come from my quest? Why was I still choking on the debilitating questions of my life?

Though it had become clear that I had to make some hard choices, I had no experience in taking charge. In desperation, I turned again to the Foundation; they referred me to Dr. Irene Hickman, an analyst in a neighboring city, who herself had gone through the same LSD program. For over a year, I made the hour's trip to her office; my husband and I saw it as our final bid to solve the increasing problems we were having. We had to exorcise this demon, this monkey on my back, and maybe save what was left of our marriage.

I went to Dr. Hickman wanting to understand how I could live as the "survivor" if this demon died; pain seemed to be the common denominator in both dimensions of the "artist/ woman" dichotomy and I was tired beyond words of living with it. As a framework for our discussions, I took to Dr. Hickman copies of the series of drawings I had done for the Foundation (see Drawings 1-18). I wanted to understand their significance, to elicit some meaning and direction for my life.

Through hypnotherapy sessions, and using the drawings, one by one as a catalyst, I was guided to some deeply moving and revealing experiences. But again, I found words inadequate to describe them; Dr. Hickman suggested I try drawing out the experience, as I had done for the Foundation. When I returned home after each session, I went to my drawing tablet and my pen. In the same intensely focused altered state that had become my "tool" in the LSD drawings, I drew out the images, so that Dr. Hickman could see the inner condition they revealed.

The first image I made (see Drawing 19), described my feeling of not being able to breathe, a condition that had recurred periodically throughout my marriage and had, also, surfaced during my LSD session. Through regression techniques, we traced this feeling back to what seemed to be a birth trauma which, to my astonishment, my mother later verified. She had tried, she said, to "hold me back," squeezing her legs tightly together while en route to the hospital; but I was born, despite her efforts, there in the taxicab, just as it was reaching the parking lot of the hospital in San Francisco.

With Dr. Hickman's guidance, I realized that the LSD experience itself was a kind of birth trauma, the birth of parts of me that had been "held back", parts I'd been afraid to know about and claim and that had tried to claw their way out of their dark places to breathe in the light.

Drawing 19

Drawing 20

Drawing 21

Drawing 22

Drawing 23

Drawing 24

Drawing 25

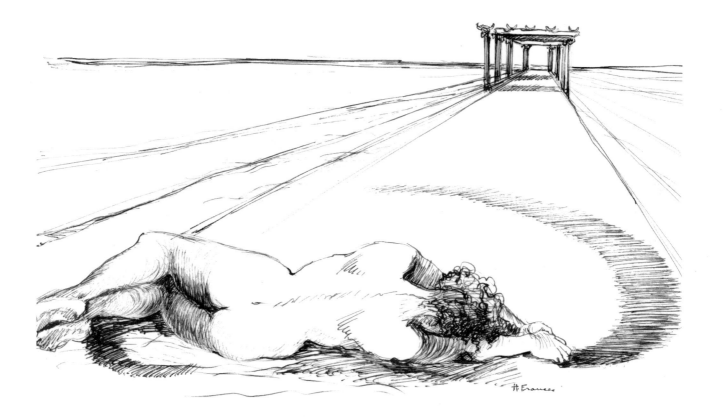

Drawing 26

Drawing 27

Drawing 28

Drawing 29

Drawing 30

Drawing 31

Drawing 32

Drawing 33

Drawing 34

Drawing 35

Drawing 36

Drawing 37

SECTION 3. The Return Trip

My Truth and its Consequences

From the drawings I had done for Dr. Hickman (see Series 2, Drawings 19-37), I had a few more insights. They showed me how deeply I felt I had failed my culture's expectations of its good Greek daughters and wives, how convinced I was that I was not the helpmate but the destroyer of my husband's dreams, his serenity, his health, our marriage and our children. I bought this image of myself as "destroyer" lock, stock and barrel, and, early in my married life, guilt and depression had triggered a desperate attempt through sleeping pills to put an end to the overwhelming burden. Though I was not successful in that attempt, it was an escape route I tried several times again during my marriage, because I could not think of any other way to end the warring factions inside me. These were, indeed, desperate solutions that had caused considerable pain to everyone around me, created more guilt and solved nothing. In these drawings, it is easy to see how deeply the tension was rooted in my psyche and how ominously it grew—seemingly, in direct proportion to the distance from my own basic rhythm that the expectations of my marriage, and my culture, imposed upon me.

It was obvious that I had to take on the overwhelming responsibility of reshaping my life in a more consonant direction. Though I had made some changes in my life, it was now time for the hardest move of all. Shortly after I completed the last drawing in this series, I knew it was not possible for John and me to continue to live with the sadness and confusion that had become our lives. It seemed there was no alternative but to end our marriage, and through a blur of fear and pain, the necessary steps were taken. I moved back to the San Francisco Bay Area, where I had lived before my marriage. The year was 1965, two years past the LSD experience, but still not past the echoes of those long-term conflicts.

In this series of drawings, it is not difficult to see the oppressive weight of the cultural expectations and the conflicts they precipitated. They show the swing between two worlds, the tightrope I walked, the almost audible loneliness of the figure being pulled (or guided?) down a path of canvas, in an emotionally powerful way (see Drawings 36-37). It is in this series of drawings that the fleshed-out bull first surfaces, though there is the suggestion of its horns in the shadow behind the figure in the earlier drawing (see Drawing 37) and in the crescent shapes that recur in later drawings – perhaps as Protean messengers, foretelling my future encounters with the same enemy?

There are certain recurring crescent shapes that serve as cast shadows in this series. They interest me as an artist because I recognize that often these shapes have no relationship to the figures or objects that cast these shadows. They recur consistently in this series and alter themselves only slightly in many of the subsequent series.

There is, in this series, for the first time, a dramatic shift from passivity to action, to a dangerous and savage rage. The bull first drags the unresisting body to the edge of a precipice; later the figure turns on him in an explosive slashing. Great wounds are inflicted, and blood is spilled. In an excess of fury and venom, a figure is impaled on a painter's palette by a woman whose visage and body are distorted and frightening to look upon (see Drawing 32).

From those drawings, it is evident that I was still in mortal combat, on the psychic level, with my enemy, the "demon art". This demon was pitted against my marriage and against the "good" part of me, the one who wanted peace and an end to the destruction and unhappiness of her marriage and her world. In the murderous fury with which the figure with a Medusa's head spears her enemy (see Drawing 32) lies testimony to how savagely and destructively my loyalties were divided. And the terrible guilt and depression I had carried for so long, for making art a priority over domestic pursuits, is eloquently revealed in the drawing depicting my two children on either side of a box (see Drawing 28). The box contains a despairing huddled figure, and on top of the box are perched the dramatic symbols of the figure's agony and guilt: paint brushes sharing a space with death. In my guilty assessment at that time, I had placed not only myself but my children in the shadow of death, in pursuit of my art career; and the feeling in that drawing was that I alone had placed us there, I alone carried the responsibility. The part of me that had been "forbidden" to live, the persistent demon, art, had insisted on exacting this unbearable penalty.

In a very eloquent way, the drawings address the duality, dichotomy and deception that had become my life at that time: two women occupied my body and spoke through my spirit, and the despair of each was unendurable. When one carried the other, the weight bent her down. When one was pierced with pain, the other wept too. The "horns" of my dilemma are quite literal in these drawings.

This series attests, in a way that saddens me still, to the damage I had sustained, to the divided loyalties of my life, to the polarization of my directives, and to the seemingly irreconcilable and limited alternatives I deemed available to me. This series also points to the deeply seated guilt I carried for the repercussions my struggle visited on my husband and children.

These drawings remind me how long I lived with that duality, the two women weeping in their separate corners and wringing their hands in the rooms of my life. One of them was "good", the other "bad", and neither seemed to have the upper hand. I needed the approval my culture lavished on its "good" women; and I needed, beyond reason or approval, to consort with my demon, my "bad" self, my powerful, primitive beast in whose company I played out the unspent passions of my life. The drawings show that I felt it was this same beast that also tortured, tantalized and invaded me and made my life unendurable. This was the beast I had to silence at all costs, so I could live a normal life and be at peace. They also show how unequal that battle was: at one point, I impaled the enemy with a spear and another time slashed him with a dagger; but he had a Protean ability to change form, so that I faced the same encounter many times. And each time, although it was I who struck and drew blood, it was also I whose face was contorted with pain, and the blood I was spilling was mine.

From my present vantage point, I see the contradictory aspects of that old struggle, the inner meaning of that bull that I drew over and over. For so long, I had let myself become a victim of the male view of the nature of woman—and for so long I had been a reactor to the conditions of my life. I now see that this posture of passivity was killing me. I see the paradox between my outwardly passive stance and the underlying turmoil in my psyche.

I believe the bull, who in my drawings shook me and dragged me and chained me and menaced me, represents the denied, rejected and despised part of me, the powerful force, the unacceptable virility of my own creative drive. I think it represents the strong woman, the rejected animus, the vital strength and purpose that I wasn't able to acknowledge, let alone claim or use, in that context of my life and at that stage of my awareness and development. I had not yet learned to endure the world I lived in, let alone act upon it.

There might, of course, be other aspects as well, passed along to me, perhaps, with the race memory, or the genes of my Cretan heritage. Maybe there are aspects of the Minotaur, or as suggested to me by a friend, of the great bull Taurus who bore the goddess Europa across the seas to Crete.

Had I activated the race memory in some mysterious way? Was I reliving the pattern of some former life? Or had I simply depicted how the collective mind of modern woman perceives the male?

SECTION FOUR. Endings

Death in the Family

This series (Drawings 38-42) was done almost ten years later, in 1974, when my father died. The five drawings that came out of that encounter with his death have some powerful and uncanny connections with the ones that have gone before. Some shapes recur, and new shapes appear. Although I was dealing with loss and grief, it is now my understanding that these drawings contain some symbols of hope and renewal. In Drawing 38, for instance, there is an infant, holding a winged creature, amid ruins, death and decay. Certainly, at the time of their execution, I was feeling far from hopeful. These symbols appeared, nevertheless. The child appears again (see Drawing 40), this time inviting eye contact. Its body is pressed against a root system and tree branches, a torso crowned by my father's face, around which is a circle of grief and love.

The most enigmatic and fascinating of this series is the complex and elegant intertwining above the head of the figure representing me (see Drawing 42). There was, for me, a sense of powerful release from grief when this image was completed.

These drawings, each taking up to a day to render, were, like all the other drawings in these series, a meditative activity. The meandering of my pen was a contemplative process into which years of memories and impressions were distilled and slowly drawn out. As I had done before, I took myself away to a quiet place, where I would be undisturbed and private, and where I could lose myself in this kind of reverie. I spent those five days dealing with my father's death in an almost deserted boatel-cottage, in wintertime, bent over my drawing pad silently grieving in this particular way. The drawings are dense, dark and almost audibly desolate. But at the end of those five days, with five completed drawings, the healing process had begun.

I could go home.

Drawing 38

Drawing 39

Drawing 40

Drawing 41

Drawing 42

Love and Separation

Almost two years after my father's death, a long-term relationship with Allen, a man whom I deeply loved, disintegrated. My trust had been most painfully betrayed and I plunged into a dark and long-lasting depression, facing a severe crisis once again. I needed to make sense of the chaotic feelings and pull myself out of my dangerous depression. I went again to the boatel-cottage with my drawing pad, my bottle of ink, and my pen—my "therapeutic tools" to cure what ailed me, or at the very least, to start me on my way.

When I looked at these drawings in this series some time later, I was struck by the explicit sexual imagery. Sex had indeed been a joyful part of that relationship, so that was not the information I needed. Was I, once again, relying too much on the male? Was I relying too much on what was pleasurable and not paying enough attention to what was not working in the relationship? If so, what were my own motives in keeping myself in that situation? I knew I had deliberately downplayed some of the negative, and hurtful, aspects of this man, telling myself "it probably wouldn't happen again", or that he would change… was I not willing to see him clearly? Where in these drawings would I find what I was looking for?

There were indeed additional clues, but I did not see them. Perhaps because I wasn't willing or ready yet to see. I found them quite easily many months later, but not in time to keep me from resuming the relationship. Even though I was learning to trust in whatever guidance I could interpret in the drawings I had done since the LSD series, there seemed to be periods where either I ignored it or couldn't/wouldn't see it. I was too blinded by the attraction to see what the drawings were bringing to my attention.

In this series, there was a clear indication that however significant this relationship had come to be, my authentic direction was away from that relationship. This is especially evident in the drawing in which a female figure is apparently running for her life, springing out of a circled formation of hands, bodies, and breasts (see Drawing 44).

Apparently, in this relationship, I was stuck in the "lower chakras". A strange new face, a devilish sort of figure, appears in the interlocking circle of figures in that same drawing. He might or might not be an outgrowth of a similar figure, first appearing twenty years earlier in one of my drawings in Series 2 (see Drawing 25). Or he might or might not be an aspect of Pan, who, I understand, in some cultures represents a positive image of sexuality. The joy— and the menace—which surfaced in these drawings were something that I experienced in a very real way in this relationship.

In this series I am also struck by the suggestion that my "higher self" had very little voice in this relationship, or perhaps, was intentionally ignored. This is the reading I give to Drawing 49, which depicts a powerful female figure who is unable to fly because someone has a grip on her lower torso and is pulling her down. Through her torn flesh, her insides are visible up to her heart level. She seems poised for flight, her body turned away from seven luminous circles on top of which a serpent crests—but her gaze remains riveted on the serpent, and there is a sadness in her face as her torso turns away.

In reviewing this series, I find much to contemplate in the complexity of the imagery; much, in retrospect, to think about in the depiction of genitalia gone amuck, becoming mouths tinged with menace, teeth bared, capable of unimaginable harm. There is a sense of severely conflicted emotions, of energies perilously out of balance. There is also detailed imagery focusing on nurturing, holding, mending—a fairly accurate summation of the role I played in this relationship.

From where I am today, I can see the cryptic guidance in these images, unavailable to me at that time, at that level of my awareness. Even if I had seen it, I no doubt would not have acted on it.

It seems I had to learn the same lessons all over again—I was not going to be an "easy study". And so, after a brief period of separation, I resumed the relationship, riding an emotional roller coaster until our final—and violent—break-up, four years later.

Drawing 43

Drawing 44

Drawing 45

Drawing 46

Drawing 47

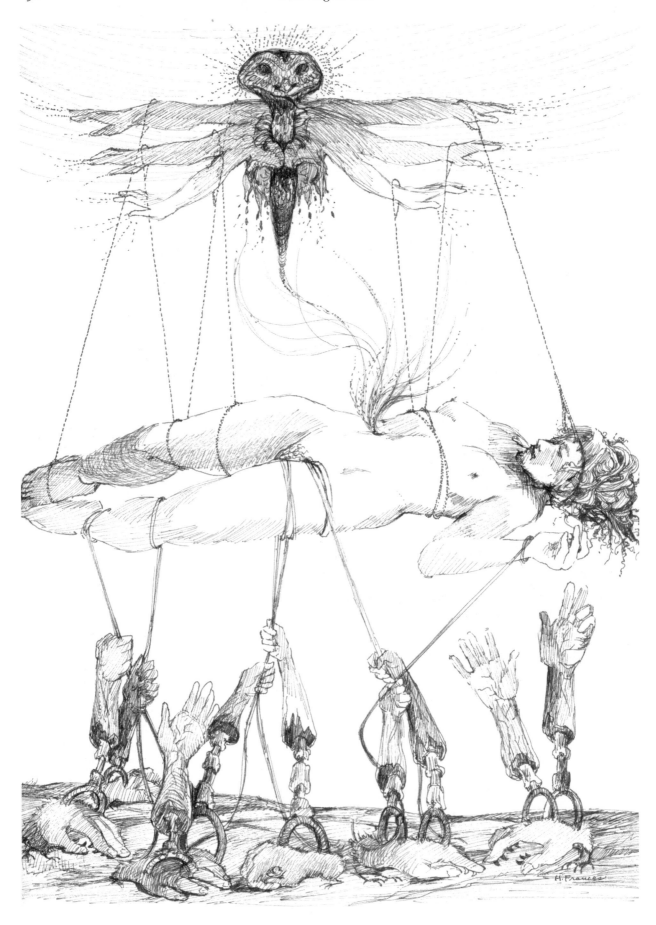

Drawing 48

Drawing 49

Creative Blocks

There are three drawings in this series, dealing with two separate occasions of severe creative blocks experienced within a short interval in 1980.

Though I had gone through fallow periods before in my creative life, these two episodes, occurring as they did during the very difficult year before my relationship finally ended, seemed harder to bear than usual. In addition, this uncreative period seemed to last an inordinately long time, long enough to push my panic button. I had come to the frightening conclusion that I would never be able to draw or paint again and that everything in my creative life was over.

I thought it would be helpful to take myself away so I could be alone with the pain of that blocked condition, and perhaps, in the silence, I would find it easier to bear. And so I checked myself into a San Francisco motel, on a quiet street, off the tourist track.

Out of past habit on my solitary treks, I took with me my drawing tablet, pen and ink. It was hard not to be intimidated by what they implied; they were, after all, an artist's tools. I was certain, in my heart of hearts, that I was no longer an artist. The well of ideas, for me, had run dry and my skills had deserted me. The art career, for which I had sacrificed the happiness of so many others, was over. What would sustain me in the years to come, if not art? What identity was mine, if not that of an artist? It was a grim and depressing time.

These three drawings are the result of facing that issue. Though the paradox escaped me at the time, the fact is that while I was in an empty uncreative state—a block—I created three drawings that described that condition. As they say, "go figure".

Everything in these drawings is stagnant, unmoving, rigid; stone becomes a good metaphor and abounds in the drawings. In Drawing 50, a lifeless infant lies on a slab of stone, its body a column of stone separated into pieces. Ghostly heads of elephants eerily float under arches (or are they teeth?) of stone. The only "animation" comes from the open mouth of the figure trapped in columns of stone; it seems to be sounding an endless silent scream. In Drawing 51, veins and tubes run from the massively bulging center of the head back inward and into the body from which they grow, and nothing seems to be "coming out". I now can see evidence, however, suggested by the active threading of roots and veins between the figure and the sprouting form on which she sits, that much was happening internally, a creative exchange was still going on.

In Drawing 52, though the figure is huddled and bare, it is being held in the embrace of a tree already bearing flowers.

Complex themes run through these three powerful drawings, quietly working in an amazing way to break the paralyzing block and see me through that depressing time.

These drawings were, and are, a potent reminder to me that the creative process is indeed a process—an ongoing, underlying continuum, never absent, holding flowers ready to bloom. They have helped me to trust the fallow times as well as the harvest.

Drawing 50

Drawing 51

Drawing 52

SECTION FIVE: Seeing Through the Drawings

Unchained

The last series here deals with the second and final stage of the break-up of the relationship with Allen, referred to in Section Four. It came when I could no longer deceive myself about his drinking, which fueled a dangerous temper…not when it finally erupted into physical violence.

The healing of my body came quickly but the healing of my spirit took a lot longer—and it came through my drawing tablet, to which I ultimately turned for guidance.

The predominant tone in this series is one of healing, forgiveness, and some residual anger, though it is tempered with compassion. This is instantly readable in the first drawing (see Drawing 53): the hand that holds the knife seems tentative in its intention; and the hand that holds the infant lover makes a protective cradle close to the nurturing breast.

The love and forgiveness I read into these drawings seems also to extend to the figure representing me (see Drawing 55). I believe these drawings graphically detail my own path towards healing from the pain of that final separation.

In Drawing 54, the horizon of breasts alludes to the nurturing part of me that was always very active in this particular relationship, although from my present vantage point, "enabling" might be a more enlightened interpretation. Arms and hands in many of the other series are harder to interpret; in one drawing (see Drawing 47), a lioness has hands and the man astride her has claws. And, perhaps as a nod to my wishful thinking at the time, there is a merging of bodies sharing a pair of wings.

In this final series, the sexual aspect of this relationship is again referred to: in Drawing 56, the male figure is chained by his penis. In Drawing 57, the figure representing me is shown chained to the penis of the prone male figure—and the female is embodied in the bull. This seems to eloquently reveal to me that my own virility, the strongest part of me (i.e., the "bull"), was chained, made helpless—again, by a dependency on the man in my life.

The last drawing in this series is an intentionally playful one, in which I acknowledge my gratitude to the makers of the drawing ink I was using at the time. Despite its playful overtones, however, it sums up the release and termination of those life-changing experiences, which covered a span of some twenty years. It serves as a reminder to me that through these pen-and-ink drawings, I was able to confront, articulate, record, and see the journey of discovery and learning that enabled me to come to terms with some of the more painful episodes of my life. These drawings taught me more about myself than all the years of therapy ever had, and they continue to do that even now.

Since the time of the last drawing in 1980, I have not felt the need to add to this drawing journal. This is not because I've have had no additional crises in my life, nor suffered additional pain and loss, nor made wrong choices or great mistakes. Rather it's because I believe I have a keener ear now, for that inner guide. I know the value of listening inwardly, and especially, the importance of taking mindful action. And even though the pathway at times is dark, I can see my way more clearly in the shadows because I am not so afraid to look.

Drawing 53

Drawing 54

Drawing 55

Drawing 56

Drawing 57

Drawing 58

Drawing 59

Drawing 60

Drawing 61

The Healing Dialogue

It has been over thirty-five years since that March morning when I set out for my appointment at the Foundation, hoping to find "revelations on the head of a pin", solutions in a speck of LSD. As I write this, I am aware of the positive changes in my life since my journey began that long-ago March morning; I am also aware now, in looking back, of how greatly they were facilitated by my sometimes timely, sometimes belated, study of these 61 drawings.

It struck me, as I reviewed them for this book, how each drawing "understood" me better than I consciously understood myself, and how this understanding was imparted through my visual senses, though unavailable to my rational mind. Each time I had reached an impasse in my life, the drawings intuited the path ahead and offered guidance and direction, in a healing dialogue with pen and paper.

With this view of myself from the inside out, afforded by the drawings, I had a tiny aperture to look into the world of the creative unconscious and elicit its meaning for me, keeping in touch with my own inner reality so that I could be better equipped to deal with the outer. In this way, I had a better chance for survival on my own terms, and I could place myself in a more authentic way in the world.

From my perspective now, as a woman making my independent way in the world, I see how truly slowly this authentic place came about—how each step forward had its concomitant three steps back. The habits of my mind, which dictated the habits of my life, were, and still are, hard to break, hard to set in new directions, no matter how compelling those directions are. It was frustrating to find that what I learned, what I created from my learning, the sometimes grace of my mind and spirit—had to be re-learned and recreated, not once but many times. But each fresh start was always from a closer vantage point to my goal of conscious living—and from a better, more vital context for reaching it.

The speck of psychoactive chemical that, in 1963, had blasted the sensory centers of my mind, had also blasted open the doors to my growth, healing and spiritual awareness, which I believe is in the record of these drawings. They remain for me the best record of how the creative force reveals, illuminates, transforms and integrates the workings of the subconscious mind. They affirm the validity of the use of the unconscious as a way of making sense of our behavior and our personal worlds. And they are a visual witness to that inner voice that, over the years, I have better attuned my ear to hear—the primitive, creative intelligence that I believe intuitively directs us to the healthiest expression of our most authentic selves.

These drawings are the visible record of my own path towards a still-evolving Self. They have been my most potent healers, my truest guides and greatest teachers on this constantly unfolding path. ◆

AFTERWORD

Image and Archetype

The artist says "I seem to have touched upon a universal journey and an underlying collective memory". Her statement is provocative, challenging us to envision that collective and universal memory. Carl Jung's conceptualization of the archetypes as sources of universal motifs, forming a collective human psychological inheritance, may aid us in our effort to grasp the experience depicted here. Archetypal patterns emerge both in individual images and in collective folklore. For the purpose of deepening our understanding of Frances' journey we will use Estella Lauter's methodological distinction between archetype and archetypal image, in which she suggests that "we continue to use the concept of the archetypal image to identify images with recurrent attraction and the concept of the archetype to refer to the tendency to form images, in relationship to patterns of development that are widespread and relatively constant through the centuries.....the archetypal images would be our sole means of inferring the presence of archetypes". (1985, p. 49) The images here certainly meet the criterion of recurrent attraction, meaning that they reflect motifs which people in innumerable cultures and over many ages have used for the depiction of transformative processes.

There are innumerable images in the first journey record which reflect developmental patterns that are traceable in ancient myth and ritual. The overall structure of separation, descent to some version of the land of the dead, and return, which is readily discernible in the record, is an archetypal hero's journey. (Campbell, 1968) Such a journey is typically under-taken for personal and cultural renewal. Experiences of skeletal dismemberment (like those depicted in Series 1, images 2-4) are an aspect of crossing over into the underworld that appear in the earliest known versions of hero journeys, those in which a tribal shaman enters an alternative reality in order to seek special healing or balancing knowledge. Shamans frequently used hallucinogenic substances to facilitate these spirit journeys and were inspired to develop ritual practices, which would preserve and build on the insights afforded by the journey. In much the same way Frances developed a ritual practice of drawing which she could use to return to her source of balance and renewal without the use of a drug.

Although this pattern is ancient, recurrent and widespread, it is, in most literature, male-identified—the archetypal hero's journey. The journey we seek to understand is, on the other hand, essentially female. Conquest, dragon slaying and trophy taking play no part here. Coming back to the pivotal images of dismemberment, how can we understand this process as a female descent?

Tiamat and Inanna

Female dismemberment occurs in mythic narrative in two radically different forms. We can use the myths of Tiamat and Inanna to exemplify these two forms. Tiamat was a great Babylonian goddess, "she who fashions all things". She was defeated in battle by Marduk, a god, hero and avenger of "the fathers". "Where after he split her like a shellfish, in two halves: set one above as a heavenly roof…He then established a great abode, the Earth." (Campbell, 1991) Marduk goes on to order and rule all that Tiamat had made and all that was made from her mutilated body. Tiamat's dismemberment provides the prima materia for a new patriarchal world. She is sacrificed and destroyed in the process, her very body converted to serve the ambitions of the patriarchal heroic ideal.

Inanna was the Sumerian "Queen of Heaven and Earth". Her dismemberment occurs in the course of an underworld journey, which she voluntarily undertakes. Her initiation into the underworld requires her to be stripped. At each of the seven gates of the great below, Inanna is forced to give up another of her earthly attributes until she is a slab of meat rotting on a peg, a process reminiscent of crucifixion. Her dismemberment is an integral aspect of her encounter and reconciliation with the "dark sister" Ereshkigal, ruler of the underworld and a Goddess of death and regeneration. Inanna undergoes a necessary deconstruction of her old configuration of self. She is re-embodied and returns from the descent with a new stance toward her upper world life, a stance which allows her to reconfigure her connection to the masculine powers of the upper world, represented in the myth by her consort Dumuzi. Her dismemberment has occurred in the service of her own regeneration.

Frances' journey incorporates both forms of female dismemberment. She describes her marriage as a battlefield, with conflict raging over her commitment to art, and she had attempted suicide several times as a solution to her inability to be the kind of woman she and her husband thought she should be. She began then in the place of Tiamat, with her creative body, her artist self, torn apart in the service of a patriarchal worldview. Her voluntary descent, through the LSD experience, into the cauldron of the unconscious shifted her dismemberment experience to one reflecting the underworld initiation of Inanna. She is stripped of her flesh, (See Drawing 5) and spends her time on the cross (See Drawing 12). These are all necessary steps in the process of profound change, deconstruction leading to renewal. Frances states "I found…my death, the total disintegration of my sense of self, the reintegration of which…is still going on". This dismemberment in the underworld leads to rebirth, as did Inanna's.

According to Sylvia Perera, a Jungian analyst, Inanna's journey is the archetypal model of a process, which is particularly important to women who have tried to form themselves in a patriarchal mold. She perceives the process as "an initiation essential for most modern women in the Western world; without it we are not whole. The process requires both a sacrifice of our identity as spiritual daughters of the patriarchy and a descent….because so much of the power and passion of the feminine has been dormant in the underworld—in exile for five thousand years". (1981, p. 14) Frances' descent functioned as an initiation into wholeness for her as an individual, leading to the retrieval of exiled aspects of herself: it also reflected a collective situation for women, who were and are struggling with the divisions within self and world created by patriarchal culture.

The record of the first journey shares another feature with the descent of Inanna, in that both Inanna and Frances emerge from the underworld through the intervention of helpful male figures. Enki, the God of Wisdom, by sending his emissary's to the underworld to aid Inanna, takes the step that catalyzes her re-embodiment and return. Similarly a male figure, seemingly an emissary from an open horizon of paint colors (See Drawing 9) reaches out to raise Frances back into the upper world. Then a flame-winged bird (See Drawing 10) restores her flesh. These two images are typical symbols of the masculine spirit guide, the animus, which is pivotal to the view of female individuation put forward by Jung sixty years ago.

The Animus

The notion that it is normal for a woman to experience and develop masculine aspects of herself is now widely accepted. Simply put these masculine aspects form the animus, the "inner man". The concept of the animus is controversial, however, particularly among feminists. A major difficulty with Jung's theory comes from his portrayal of the animus as an embodiment of stereotypical masculine traits, such as assertiveness, rationality, control and abstraction. He touts that portrayal as a description of an eternal, universal and archetypal masculinity (all of this is mirrored in his theoretical construct of the anima in men); Jung showed little awareness of the impact of culture on the construction of gender traits. Consequently his theory came to resemble a form of biological determinism, with all of that notion's oppressive history and potential.

Many efforts have been made by post-Jungian writers to disentangle the concept of the animus from its problematic aspects. They have expended this intellectual effort in part because animus figures continue to take significant roles in women's dreams and symbolic expressions. The animus is an aspect of the unconscious, which mediates between the ego and the depths of a woman's inner world. Mediation, in this sense, means that a masculine figure or image facilitates and guides the relationship between different parts of the self. In the drawings of Series 1 we can readily see masculine figures engaged in both helpful (See Drawing 9, in which the man is reaching down to aid in her ascent) and hurtful (See Drawing 13, in which the husband/boulder crushes her) mediating action. Frances' relationship to her artist-self is being supported by a positive animus figure in the first instance and punished by a negative animus figure in the second.

The key to what is still useful to women about the concept of the animus lies in this function of mediation. It may be that for women who are saturated by patriarchal values the mediation provided by masculine symbolic figures is necessary to the process of making a viable relationship to the "phenomenon of difference". (Samuels, 1985, p. 136) When a woman is identified with the conventional gender role she relates to different, unconventional aspects of the self through internalized masculine complexes which are repressive and scathingly critical, like the husband/boulder which crushes the impulse toward art in Drawing 13 from Series 1. In this way the internal values, which guide the individual personality, reflect the repressive way in which patriarchal culture responds to difference, to the "other". This negative mediation must be consciously confronted and brought to awareness before a constructive relationship can develop between the ego and the "other" within. For many women, positive mediation, as depicted in Drawing 9, must happen initially through masculine figures that act as a counterbalance to the negative internalizations. This may be only a stage, but a vital one in changing the nature of the connection with exiled parts of the self. We can see these processes continuing in the bull, father and Allan images which occur in the post-LSD drawings. All of these figures play an important part in changing the relationship between Frances and her inner, repressed self, the artist "other".

The journeys depicted here not only transformed the nature of the connection between Frances and her artist-self but also connected her to an archetypal source of transformative imagery. Our hyper-rational culture does not perceive the transformative resources of the unconscious as legitimate and so there are no approved cultural activities, which mediate a connection to those resources. Consequently, each individual must discover her own relationship to this exiled part of the self, her own internal mediators. The drawing process and its visionary products provided this for Frances.

Medea's Cauldron

Jung felt that visionary works of art have an impact analogous to participation mystique, which is the phenomenon of experiencing a personal identification, a "oneness" with the transpersonal. The transpersonal may be embodied in a group, in nature or in spiritual experience. "In works of art of this nature…It cannot be doubted that the vision is a genuine primordial experience….It is not something derived or secondary, it is not symptomatic of something else, it is a true symbol—that is an expression for something real but unknown." (Jung, C.W. v.15, p.94)

The image of the artist as a mystagogue who journeys into the unknown and brings back images of a different reality is not unique to Jung, but Jung placed the artist in a key role concerning the individuation of society itself. The artist's work, if it is inspired by the "real but unknown", serves as a compensating dream, balancing the conscious attitude of an entire culture with images of unacknowledged aspects of both self and world, aspects for which consciousness does not have ready words. Jung suggested that we allow a work of visionary art to "act upon us as it acted upon the artist". (Ibid. p.105) What might that mean in relationship to Frances' drawings? How did they act upon her? How might they act upon us?

Frances describes the way in which these drawings connect her inner and outer worlds. By making a personal relationship to the archetypal images in this narrative of drawings the viewer may activate a parallel process in herself. My own relationship to the drawings has centered around the image of the cauldron. This association was prompted by a combination of things. The openings at the top of the drawings in the first series gave me the feeling of a vessel. The images are composed of stirring, swirling parts (See Drawing 2 as an example), boiling with energy, cooking into a rich, nurturing stew where meat falls off of bones and paintings liquefy. This evoked for me a bubbling cauldron in which the mixture of disparate images produces new forms. That association connected in my mind with Frances' Greek heritage and soon I was thinking about Medea's cauldron of regeneration.

When I read this statement of Frances'—"I had failed… my culture's expectations of its good Greek daughters and wives and I was…the destroyer of my husband's dreams, his serenity, our marriage and our children"—and when she states that by continuing to paint she "had somehow placed my children in the shadow of death", it seemed that she saw herself much as Euripides saw Medea. Medea is portrayed in the famous play as an unnatural, demonic woman who abandons her proper role and betrays her family for selfish, vain reasons.

Medea is the first recorded witch in Western literature and a famously bad wife and mother. She was the daughter of the King of Colchis, a sorceress and priestess of Hecate, who fell in love with Jason and helped him to carry off the Golden fleece. Medea's magic arts, desperately needed by the Argonauts at many junctures in their adventure, included the use of a fabulous cauldron of regeneration from which dismembered, stewed animals and people could be reborn with new power and vigor. After ten years of marriage Jason deserted Medea for another Princess. According to the classical version of the myth Medea killed her children and her rival, burned down her palace and flew away in a dragon chariot. Medea never died but rules in the Elysian fields, the land of the dead.

Mythographers and poets (like Robert Graves) see Medea in terms that differ greatly from her portrayal in classic Greek drama. From their point of view, her cauldron of regeneration, dragon chariot and her immortality as a Queen in the underworld may be important remnants of a divine origin myth. She may, originally, have been a Goddess of death and regeneration, probably associated with the moon in both its light and dark aspects.

The primordial motif of the Destroyer/Regenatrix portrays, in female imagery, the linked cosmic forces of destruction and creation. (Gimbutas, 1989) These forces were working in tandem in Frances' conscious life; the creative drive to paint was inextricably bound up with her experience of personal destruction. We can see destruction and creative regeneration at work together in many of the universal, cosmic images from her underworld journeys. The feminine forms of the paradoxically joined powers of death and regeneration have long been exiled to the underworld, as we saw in the story of Inanna and her descent to recover connection to Ereshkigal, the "dark sister" of death and regeneration. Frances was intimately involved with these powers and her culture provided her with no functional way of containing, or processing them. Fortunately, the LSD research project, in combination with her art, ultimately provided the necessary process and container.

Frances moved away from her emotional identification with the witch-mother/demon-wife that is analogous to Medea's usual image. The artist began to pursue an experience of the process embodied by the ancient goddess Medea's cauldron of regeneration. This is a process lost to everyday culture but apparently still accessible in the unconscious. The cauldron of regeneration is an archetypal image of ancient lineage, appearing in Celtic as well as Mediterranean myth, which provides us with a way to picture a mysterious and powerful process of fragmentation and renewal. Grasping and picturing this process requires the recovery of a primordial image because Western culture has virtually no picture or concept of destruction as necessary or potentially fruitful.

The Western deification of progress and perfect order leaves little room for the messy reality of natural cycles of creation and destruction. This dualistic, split worldview creates absolute good (objectivity, progress, control, light) and absolute evil (subjectivity, decay, chaos, dark). These absolutes are associated with and projected onto social groups in ways that have both cultural and personal implications.

Women, and other disenfranchised groups, tend to bear the projection of the deep cultural shadow that is created by the obsessive emphasis, in the West, on the absolute value of transcendence, light and perfect control. The forces of, and connections between, destruction and regeneration have been feminized and simultaneously demonized in patriarchal culture. Women as a group and as individuals are perceived as embodiments of chaotic destruction, particularly when they slip out of conventional roles and expectations, as Frances did. The imagery and story of Medea's cauldron resurrects a non-dualistic experience of destruction and regeneration; it gives us a way to conceptualize and feel the fruitful connections between fragmentation and rebirth.

Cyclical Journeys

I have not touched upon numerous important questions in this discussion. Frances documents six journeys to the unconscious. After the sixth use of the drawing process Frances no longer felt the need to actively engage in the process, although she continued to use the existing drawings as sources of guidance and inspiration. This essay has only addressed the imagery in the first series and has not done a comprehensive survey of that. What about the many other rich archetypal symbols that recur and develop in this record? How can we understand the fact that the impact of the drawings, on the artist and on the viewer, does not seem to depend on an intellectual decoding of the symbolism? This discussion will conclude by addressing these questions.

The LSD experience gave Frances access to a powerful aspect of her psyche. That aspect, the unconscious, has its own timeline and, as we have said, one of its purposes is to balance conscious life. The ways in which Frances' life and experience of self were split at the time of the first journey were not entirely resolved by her journeys to the unconscious. However, these six journeys created a bridge, a viable relationship between waking, everyday life and the artist within, a relationship which was no longer experienced as annihilating but as life-giving. Once the split was healed to that extent, a special process or container was no longer needed and the natural self-regulating processes of the psyche could take over.

One can be profoundly and authentically impacted by Frances' narrative of transformation without identifying and explicating each significant archetypal theme in the record. In fact, such a project might well prove impossible to complete. The multileveled nature of the unconscious and the multivalent nature of symbols are not adequately addressed by such a linear process. Reductionistic decoding and categorical assessments of transformative images tend to strip them of their visceral power, ignoring the way in which such images impact the self through multiple ways of knowing.

I have employed a method of personal and mythological association to guide my exploration of the psychological import of the drawings. This method allows a deepening of understanding and avoids reductionism. It is congruent with the associational flow of the drawing process itself. It also leaves many provocative images and symbolic themes to be amplified and explored by the reader. In the previous section I made the following statement: "By making a personal relationship to the archetypal images in this narrative of drawings the viewer may activate a parallel process in herself (meaning parallel to the drawing process)." The reader, by choosing the images which most affect her, may trace the development and elaboration of those chosen symbolic elements through the cyclical journeys documented here. By allowing personal associations to flow and by researching mythological connections, each reader will evolve a uniquely individual, yet universally rooted, web of meanings and insights in response to the drawings. In this way the drawings can act as doorways to the transformative resources of the unconscious, facilitating the ability to produce new imagery, giving access to the cauldron of regeneration that lives in everyone's unconscious.

– Tanya Wilkinson, Ph.D.

REFERENCES

Campbell, Joseph. *Hero with a Thousand Faces.* Princeton, NJ: Princeton University Press (1968).

Campbell, Joseph. *The Masks of God. Vol.4.* New York: Arkana (1991).

Gimbutas, Marija. *Gods and Goddesses of Old Europe,* Berkeley: University of California Press (1982).

Jung, C.G., *Collected Works 15,* Princeton NJ: Princeton University Press (1968).

Lauter, Estelle. *Woman as Mythmaker.* Bloomington: Indiana University Press (1985).

Perera, Sylvia. *Descent to the Goddess.* Toronto: Inner City Books (1981).

Samuels, Andrew. *Jung and the Post-Jungians.* London: Routledge (1985).

Samuels, Andrew. "Gender and Psyche", *Anima,* Vol. 11, 2; p. 136.

ABOUT THE PUBLISHER

The Multidisciplinary Association for Psychedelic Studies (MAPS) is a membership-based non-profit research and educational organization with over 1800 members and growing. We assist scientists to design, fund, conduct and report on the risks and benefits of the therapeutic, spiritual, and creative uses of psychedelic drugs and marijuana. MAPS' goal is to use the data generated from scientific research to develop these drugs into FDA-approved prescription medicines.

Can you imagine a cultural reintegration of the use of psychedelics and the states of mind they engender?

Please join MAPS in supporting the expansion of scientific knowledge in this promising area. Progress is only possible with the support of individuals who care enough to take individual and collective action.

Since 1995 MAPS has disbursed over $1-million to research and educational projects.

HOW MAPS HAS MADE A DIFFERENCE:

- Supported long-term follow-up studies of pioneering research with LSD and psilocybin from the 1950s and 1960s.
- Sponsored Dr. Evgeny Krupitsky's pioneering research into the use of ketamine-assisted psychotherapy in the treatment of alcoholism and heroin addiction.
- Opened an FDA Drug Master file for MDMA. This is required for any drug before it can be legitimately researched in the U.S.
- Assisted Dr. Charles Grob to obtain permission for the first human studies in the United States with MDMA after it was criminalized in 1985.
- Funded the world's first government-approved scientific study of the therapeutic use of MDMA (Spain).
- Sponsored the first study to analyze the purity and potency of street samples of "Ecstasy" and medical marijuana.
- Funded the successful effort of Dr. Donald Abrams to obtain permission for the first human study into the therapeutic use of marijuana in 15 years, and to secure a $1-million grant from the National Institute on Drug Abuse.
- Obtained orphan-drug designation from the FDA for smoked marijuana in the treatment of AIDS Wasting Syndrome.
- Funded the synthesis of psilocybin for the first FDA-approved study in a patient population in twenty-five years.

Benefits of MAPS Membership

As a member of MAPS, you'll receive the quarterly MAPS Bulletin. In addition to reporting on the latest research in both the U.S. and abroad, the Bulletin includes feature articles, personal accounts, book reviews, and reports on conferences and allied organizations. MAPS members are invited to participate in a vital on-line mailing list and to visit our website, which includes all articles published by MAPS since 1988.

Unless otherwise indicated your donation will be considered an unrestricted gift to be used to fund high-priority projects. If you wish, however, you may direct contributions to a specific study. Your tax-deductible donation may be made by credit card or check made out to MAPS. Gifts of stock are welcome, as are trust and estate planning options.

The MAPS list is strictly confidential and not available for purchase. The MAPS Bulletin is mailed in a plain envelope.

MAPS SUBSCRIPTION RATES

Basic Membership— $35

Student/ Low income Membership— $20

Basic Plus Membership— $50*

Supporting Membership— $100*

Patron Membership— $250+*

*(Includes a complimentary book)

International members add $15 for postage

Multidisciplinary Association for Psychedelic Studies

2105 Robinson Avenue, Sarasota, fl 34232

Tel: 941-924-MAPS (6277) or 888-868-6277

E-mail: info@maps.org

Please visit our website: www.maps.org

ORDERING INFORMATION

Drawing It Out (ISBN 0-9660019-5-8) ...$19.95/copy

Shipping and Handling Charges

Domestic book rate (allow 3 weeks): $3.00

Domestic priority mail (allow 7 days): $5.00

($1.00 each additional copy)

Overseas airmail rates (allow 10 days):

Canada/Mexico ($7.00) — Other Countries ($9.00) — Pacific Rim ($10.00)

Methods of Payment

Check or money order in U.S. Dollars, Mastercard, Visa, American Express

Wholesale Orders Welcome: Case discount: 50%

Split case discount (ten copy minimum): 40%

five to nine copies: 20%

Other ways to order Drawing It Out

Via secure credit card transaction at: orders@maps.org

Toll Free at 1-888-868-MAPS (6277)

Through your favorite local bookstore

Send Orders to:

MAPS/ Drawing It Out

2105 Robinson Avenue, Sarasota, fl 34232

voice: (941)924-6277 • fax: (941)924-6265 • e-mail: orders@maps.org

Toll-free order line: 1-888-868-MAPS (6277)